3.

The Joy of Words

*Selections of literature
expressing beauty, humor, history,
wisdom or inspiration . . .
which are a joy to read
and read again*

J. G. FERGUSON PUBLISHING COMPANY
CHICAGO

1975 Printing

Editor's Comment and Acknowledgments

SOMETIMES it seems almost futile to try to write anything new because it has all been said before—and so well said. Of course, any such defeatism must lead to a dead end of accomplishment in terms of literary effort. Fortunately for the living and those to come, there are many bright new stars on the panel of contemporary writers. They are skillfully telling the story of these eventful days and their words will be read with relish by future generations. In fact, the printed word today is so prolific, and the competition with the book, the magazine and the newspaper is so great, future generations will require anthologies in great number to know what our bright literary stars have said.

In this anthology there has been no effort to be erudite, consistent, unusual or educational. The prime purpose is to amuse by exposing the reader to many things he has read before and may wish to read again. Perhaps that poem he *had* to learn, to pass freshman English, is here. He may even enjoy rereading it under different auspices. It is not possible to include only those things that appeal to him. If he dislikes poetry in any form, we hope he will please forgive us. Some of us like the "well-turned couplet." On the other hand, there are those who love Shakespeare, but just cannot understand how his hallowed words should appear with some of the more commonplace choices that have arrived in this selection. It takes all kinds you know—and we have tried to select all kinds of literature.

Perhaps there are too many selections from writers of the past. For this, we have only this to say:

> "This is the place. Stand still, my stead,
>   Let me review the scene,
> And summon from the shadowy Past
>   The forms that once have been."

or

> "Time has laid his hand
> Upon my heart, gently, not smiting it,
> But as a harper lays his open palm
> Upon his harp, to deaden its vibrations."

We are grateful for the generous cooperation of many individuals and companies in permitting us to draw upon the very wonderful wealth of books that have been published before this. We have used many in the course of this publishing effort. It is our pleasure to list below those publishers and books from which we have selected most of this material. In the event we have inadvertently failed properly to acknowledge or have omitted acknowledgment of any material used, we shall appreciate notification so that we may correct the oversight in later editions.

Holmes Complete Poems, Houghton Mifflin Company; *Great Truths by Great Authors*, J. P. Lippincott Company; *Poems on Several Occasions*, Philip Freneau; *A Dictionary of Quotations*, by Philip Hugh Dalbiac, Thomas Nelson and Sons, Ltd.; *A Treasury of Inspiration*, by Ralph L. Woods, Thomas Y. Crowell Company; *Conduct of Life*, by Ralph Waldo Emerson, Ticknor and Fields; *Poetry of the Magyars*, by John Bowring; *The True and the Beautiful*, by John Ruskin, John Wiley and Sons; *The Complete Poetical Works of Thomas Campbell*, G. P. Putnam and Sons; *Best Loved Unity Poems*, Unity School of Christianity; *The Complete Poetry and Selected Prose of John Donne*, by Charles M. Coffin; The Modern Library; *Light From Many Lamps*, by Lillian Eichler Watson, Simon & Schuster; *The Autobiography of Will Rogers*, by Donald Day, Houghton Mifflin Company; *"Now I'll Tell One," Harry Hershfield's Book of Laughs*, Greenberg; *Familiar Quotations, Salt Water Ballads*, by John Masefield, The Macmillan Company; *An Essay Concerning Humane Understanding*, by John Locke, *The Century Cyclopedia of Names;* The Century Company; *The Writings of Henry Wadsworth Longfellow*, Riverside Press; *A Little Book of Western Verse*, Charles Scribner's Sons; *The Poems and Prose Sketches of James Whitcomb Riley*, Charles Scribner's Sons; *Personal Reminiscences of General Robert E. Lee*, by Reverend J. William Jones, D. Appleton and Company; *Poems of Sidney Lanier*, Charles Scribners Sons; *A New Dictionary of Quotations*, J. P. Lippincott & Company; *The Complete Works of*

Shakespeare, Oxford University Press; *The Speaker's Garland and Literary Bouquet*, P. Garrett and Company; *Creative America*, by Ludwig Lewisohn, Harper and Brothers; *Adventures of Huckleberry Finn*, by Mark Twain, Harper and Brothers: *The Man that Corrupted Hadleyburg*, by Mark Twain, Harper and Brothers; *The Damon Runyon Story*, by Ed Weiner, Longmans, Green and Company; *The Poems of Robert Browning*, Oxford University Press; *The Man From Vermont*, by Henry Dierkes, Eileen Baskerville; *The Compleat Angler*, by Izaak Walton, Caradoc Press; *The Poetical Works of William Cullen Bryant*, D. Appleton and Company; *Ben King's Verse*, Forbes & Company; *Jefferson Reader*, E. P. Dutton and Company; *The Bigelow Papers*, James Russell Lowell, Houghton, Mifflin and Company; *A Library of Poetry and Song*, J. B. Ford and Company: *Saddle and Song*, L. P. Lippincott Company; *A Treasury of American Folk Humor*, by James M. Tidwell, Crown Publishers, Inc.; *Treasury of Wisdom, Wit and Humor*, by Adam Wooléver, Patriot Publishing Company; *Precepts and Practice*, by Constance M. Whishaw, Samuel Bagster & Sons, Ltd.; *The Way to Wealth, by Benjamin Franklin*, Simeon Ide, The Florentine Fior di Virtu of 1491, translated into English by Nicholas Fersen, published for the Library of Congress—1953.

–T.C.J.

TABLE OF CONTENTS

Wisdom

TABLE OF CONTENTS

Humor

TABLE OF CONTENTS

Benjamin Franklin

TABLE OF CONTENTS

History

Beauty

TABLE OF CONTENTS

TABLE OF CONTENTS

Business

Longfellow

S L Clemens

Whitman

Whittier

Bryant

Holmes

Lowell

Lanier

WISDOM

Wisdom is the principal thing: — Therefore, get wisdom; and with all thy getting, get understanding.
— PROVERBS IV 7

WORDS are things, and a small drop of ink,
Falling like dew upon a thought, produces
That which makes thousands, perhaps millions,
think.

—LORD BYRON

A LONG LIFE — A GOOD LIFE

by

Thomas Jefferson

You ask if I would agree to live my seventy or rather seventy-three years over again? To which I say yea. I think with you that it is a good world on the whole; that it has been framed on a principle of benevolence, and more pleasure than pain dealt out to us. These are, indeed, (who might say nay) gloomy and hypochondriac minds, inhabitants of diseased bodies, disgusted with the present, and despairing of the future; always counting that the worst will happen, because it may happen. To these I say, how much pain have cost us the evils which have never happened! My temperament is sanguine. I steer my bark with Hope in the head, leaving Fear astern. My hopes, indeed, sometimes fail; but not oftener than the forebodings of the gloomy. There are, I acknowledge, even in the happiest life, some terrible convulsions, heavy set-offs against the opposite page of the account. I have often wondered for what good end the sensations of grief could be intended. All our other passions, within proper bounds, have a useful object. And the perfection of the moral character is, not in a stoical apathy, so hypocritically vaunted, and so untruly too, because impossible, but in a just equilibrium of all the passions. I wish the pathologists then, would tell us what is the use of grief in the economy, and of what good it is the cause, proximate or remote.

ESSAY ON MAN

at ten, a child; at twenty, wild;
at thirty, tame, if ever;
at forty, wise; at fifty, rich;
at sixty, good or never.

—Anonymous

Begin the Day with Friendliness

Frank B. Whitney

Begin the day with friendliness
    And only friends you'll find.
Yes, greet the dawn with happiness;
    Keep happy thoughts in mind.
Salute the day with peaceful thoughts,
    And peace will fill your heart;
Begin the day with joyful soul,
    And joy will be your part.

Begin the day with friendliness;
    Keep friendly all day long;
Keep in your soul a friendly thought,
    Your heart a friendly song.
Have in your mind a word of cheer
    For all who come your way,
And they will bless you too, in turn,
    And wish you "Happy day!"

Begin each day with friendly thoughts,
    And as the day goes on,
Keep friendly, loving, good, and kind,
    Just as you were at dawn.
The day will be a friendly one,
    And then at night you'll find
That you were happy all day long
    Through friendly thoughts in mind.

A SMILE

A SMILE costs nothing, but gives much. It enriches those who receive, without making poorer those who give. It takes but a moment, but the memory of it sometimes lasts forever. None is so rich or mighty that he can get along without it, and none is so poor but that he can be made rich by it. A smile creates happiness in the home, fosters good will in business, and is the countersign of friendship. It brings rest to the weary, cheer to the discouraged, sunshine to the sad, and it is nature's best antidote for trouble. Yet it cannot be bought, begged, borrowed, or stolen, for it is something that is of no value to anyone until it is given away. Some people are too tired to give you a smile. Give them one of yours, as none needs a smile so much as he who has no more to give.

Author Unknown

How soon a smile of God can change the world!
How we are made for happiness—how work
Grows play, adversity a winning fight!

ROBERT BROWNING, *In A Balcony*

"TO SNAP OUT OF IT— THINK OF OTHERS"

by DR. FREDERICK LOOMIS

"IT'S BUT little good you'll do, watering last year's crops." Yet that is exactly what I have seen hundreds of my patients doing in the past twenty-five years—watering with freely flowing tears things of the irrevocable past. Not the bittersweet memories of loved ones, which I could understand, but things done which should not have been done, and things left undone which should have been done.

I am a doctor, not a preacher; but a doctor, too, must try to understand the joys and sorrows of those who come to him. He should without preaching be able to expound the philosophy that one cannot live adequately in the present, nor effectively face the future, when one's thoughts are buried in the past.

Moaning over what cannot be helped is a confession of futility and of fear, of emotional stagnation—in fact, of selfishness and cowardice. The best way to break this vicious, morbid circle—"to snap out of it"—is to stop thinking about yourself, and start thinking about other people. You can lighten your own load by doing something for someone else. By the simple device of doing an outward, unselfish act today, you can make the past recede. The present and future will again take on their true challenge and perspective.

As a doctor I have seen it tried many, many times and nearly always it has been a far more successful prescription than anything I could have ordered from the drugstore.

Dr. Loomis's premonition came true. These words were his last, for he died soon afterward.

THE

WISH OF DIOGENES

From POEMS ON SEVERAL OCCASIONS

By PHILIP FRENEAU

*Newspaper Editor, Poet, Merchant Seaman, and
Patriot of the American Revolutionary War*

A HERMIT'S house beside a stream
With forests planted round,
Whatever it to you may seem
More real happiness I deem
Than if I were a monarch crown'd.

A cottage I could call my own
Remote from domes of care;
A little garden wall'd with stone,
The wall with ivy overgrown,
A limpid fountain near,
Would more substantial joys afford,
More real bliss impart
Than all the wealth that misers hoard,
Than vanquish'd worlds, or worlds restor'd—
Mere cankers of the heart!

Vain foolish man! how vast thy pride,
How little can thy wants supply!—
'Tis surely wrong to grasp so wide—
You act as if you only had
To triumph — not to die!

Such is the patriot's boast, wher'er we roam,
His first, best country ever is at home.
—OLIVER GOLDSMITH

RULES OF LIFE

by CONFUCIUS

Celebrated Chinese Philosopher who died 478 B.C.
He traveled extensively and wrote many maxims and books.

The rule of life is to be found within yourself,
Ask yourself constantly, "What is the right thing
to do?"
Beware of ever doing that which you are likely,
sooner or later, to repent of having done.
It is better to live in peace than in bitterness and
strife.
It is better to believe in your neighbors than to
fear and distrust them.
The superior man does not wrangle. He is firm but
not quarrelsome. He is sociable but not clannish.
The superior man sets a good example to his
neighbors. He is considerate of their feelings
and their property.
Consideration for others is the basis of a good life,
a good society.
Feel kindly toward everyone. Be friendly and
pleasant among yourselves. Be generous and
fair.

The greatest man is he who chooses the right with
invincible resolution; who resists the sorest temp-
tations from within and without; who is calmest
in storms, and whose reliance on truth, on virtue,
on God, is the most unfaltering.

—CHANNING

THE ART OF GETTING ALONG

Sooner or later a man, if he is wise, discovers that life is a mixture of good days and bad, victory and defeat, give and take.

He learns that it doesn't pay to be a sensitive soul—that he should let some things go over his head like water off a duck's back.

He learns that he who loses his temper usually loses.

He learns that all men have burnt toast for breakfast now and then, and that he shouldn't take the other fellow's grouch too seriously.

He learns that carrying a chip on his shoulder is the easiest way to get into a fight.

He learns that the quickest way to become unpopular is to carry tales and gossip about others.

He learns that most people are human and that it doesn't do any harm to smile and say "good morning" even if it is raining.

He learns that most of the other fellows are as ambitious as he is, that they have brains that are as good or better, and that hard work, and not cleverness, is the secret of success.

He learns that it doesn't matter so much who gets the credit so long as the business shows a profit.

He comes to realize that the business could run along perfectly without him.

He learns to sympathize with the youngsters coming into the business, because he remembers how bewildered he was when he first started out.

He learns not to worry when he does not make a hit EVERY time, because experience has shown if he always gives his best, his average will break pretty well.

He learns that no man ever got to first base alone and that it is only through cooperative effort that we move on to better things.

He learns that the fellows are not any harder to get along with in one place than another, and that "getting along" depends about 98 per cent on himself.　　—*Anonymous*

YOUTH

YOU GROW OLD WHEN YOU QUIT PLAYING

Oh for one hour of youthful joy!
Give back my twentieth spring!
I'd rather laugh, a bright-haired boy
Than reign a gray-beard king.

—*The Old Man Dreams,* OLIVER WENDELL HOLMES

NOBODY grows old by merely living a number of years; people only grow old by deserting their ideals. Nor is youth simply a matter of ripe cheeks and supple knees. Youth is a temper of the will; a quality of the imagination, a vigour of the emotions, and a freshness of the deep springs of life. Years may wrinkle the skin, but to give up enthusiasm wrinkles the soul.

Whether seventeen or seventy, if there is in one's heart the love of wonder, the childlike appetite of what's next, and the courage to play the game as the rules are written, that person is young.

"Men do not quit playing because they grow old; they grow old because they quit playing."

Ah, what shall I be at fifty
Should Nature keep me alive,
If I find the world so bitter
When I am but twenty-five?

—*Maud,* ALFRED LORD TENNYSON

To be seventy years young is sometimes far more cheerful and hopeful than to be forty years old. —OLIVER WENDELL HOLMES

YOUTH

by OLIVER WENDELL HOLMES

*Read at the thirty-first anniversary of
the Boston Young Men's Christian Union,
May 31, 1882.*

WHY linger round the sunken wrecks
  Where old Armadas found their graves?
Why slumber on the sleepy decks
  While foam and clash the angry waves?
Up! when the storm-blast rends the clouds,
  And winged with ruin sweeps the gale,
Young feet must climb the quivering
    shrouds,
  Young hands must reef the bursting
    sail!

Leave us to fight the tyrant creeds
  Who felt their shackles, feel their scars;
The cheerful sunlight little heeds
  The brutes that prowled beneath the
    stars.
The dawn is here, the day star shows
  The spoils of many a battle won,
But sin and sorrow still are foes
  That face us in the morning sun.

Who sleeps beneath yon bannered mound
  The proudly sorrowing mourner seeks,
The garland-bearing crowd surrounds?
  A light-haired boy with beardless
    cheeks!

'Tis time this "fallen world" should rise;
  Let youth the sacred work begin!
What nobler task, what fairer prize
  Than earth to save and Heaven to win?

*Young men soon give and soon forget affronts;
Old age is slow in both.*

SIMPLE MEDICINE: *Get Busy!*

*Do not allow idleness to deceive you; for while
you give him today, he steals tomorrow from you.*

IF YOUR enemy has injured you, or your friend deceived you; if your brightest hopes have been clouded, or your reputation blackened, pray for your enemies, and then up and be doing. Better gather field flowers, plait rushes, weed the garden, or black your own shoes, than be idle. Occupation will raise your spirit, while idleness will bring it down to the dust. Occupation will often blunt the edge of the sharpest grief, keep the body in health, and preserve the mind in comparative peace. He that is in trouble should do something to get rid of it. Something must be done, and done by yourself too, when you are in trouble, or otherwise it will stick as close to you as the skin that covers you.

The moment you feel yourself getting moody and miserable, seek Divine support by prayer, and then set yourself a task immediately, something that will compel you to exert yourself, and you will be surprised at the relief it will afford you. And especially employ yourself in doing good, and mitigating the sorrows of others: while taking a thorn from the bosom of another, you will lose that which rankles in your own. Occupation cures one half of life's troubles, and tends to mitigate the remainder.

> Never give up! If adversity presses,
> Providence wisely has mingled the cup,
> And the best counsel, in all your distresses,
> Is the stout watchword of "Never give up."
> —MARTIN F. TUPPER

WE CARVE OUR DESTINY EARLY

John Ruskin, born in London, February 8, 1819, attended Christ Church, Oxford, graduating in 1842. He studied painting under Copely, Fielding, and Harding, masters of that day. He published a volume called "Modern Painters" in 1843, aiming to prove the superiority of the modern painters over the old masters. The style and originality of views in this book established Ruskin as an art critic and author. He spent many years in Italy studying art. In later, years he lectured at both Oxford and Cambridge and was a prolific writer on social problems as well as art.

THE common plea that anything does to "exercise the mind upon," is an utterly false one. The human soul, in youth, is *not* a machine of which you can polish the cogs with any kelp or brickdust near at hand; and, having got it into working order, and good, empty, and oiled serviceableness, start your immortal locomotive at twenty-five years old or thirty, express from the Strait Gate, on the Narrow Road. The whole period of youth is one essentially of formation, edification, instruction, I use the words with their weight in them; intaking of stores, establishment in vital habits, hopes, and faiths. There is not an hour of it but is trembling with destinies,—not a moment of which, once past, the appointed work can ever be done again, or the neglected blow struck on the cold iron. Take your vase of Venice glass out of the furnace, and strew chaff over it in its transparent heat, and recover *that* to its clearness and rubied glory when the north wind has blown upon it; but do not think to strew chaff over the child fresh from God's presence, and to bring the heavenly colors back to him—at least in this world.

All of us who are worth anything, spend our manhood in unlearning the follies, or expiating the mistakes of our youth.

—SHELLEY

Leadership Needed Today

Reprinted by permission of International Business Machines Corporation, from *How You Can Influence Foreign Policy*, THINK Magazine. Copyright 1959.

Leadership is particularly important in the United States because, unlike Europe and Asia, no caste system has ever taken deep root in this country. In the older, more static civilizations, because of a long tradition of monarchical and aristocratic rule, the leader is, so to speak, often "naturally" provided. A distinguished family name, a title, a uniform – sometimes all three combined – may suffice to establish the authority and prestige. His leadership position is rarely questioned; his right to wield power or exert influence is hardly challenged. He is, in the well-known phrase, "to the manner born."

Not so in the United States. Here, the leader first has to prove himself to achieve his position, and secondly, he has to exert himself to retain it. This, in essence, is a part of America's democratic dynamism. It was recognized long ago by an early democrat, Thomas Jefferson, that democracy, by rejecting the idea and the practice of a caste system, must therefore rely on what he called a "natural aristocracy." Nature, he said, scatters human talents among all types of people, rich and poor alike, and this reservoir of abilities must be used for leadership and enrichment of democracy.

American life today exemplifies Jefferson's conception of a natural aristocracy. Whether in business or government or the professions, America's leaders are generally those whose positions were attained through individual effort and skill, rather than birth. Cases of inherited wealth and social status do exist among the leaders, but the majority, including the last two Presidents of the United States, come from modest homes. Surveys indicate that most leaders—mayors, presidents of civic organizations, members of Congress, heads of industries—are college graduates and, on community levels, more than half of them have professional degrees. The educational ladder—that is, training for positions of power and influence – still remains the primary avenue of advancement in American life.

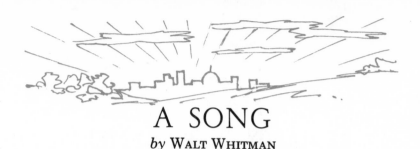

A SONG

by WALT WHITMAN

1

COME, I will make the continent indissoluble;
I will make the most slendid race the sun ever yet shone
  upon;
I will make divine magnetic lands,
    With the love of comrades,
      With the life-long love of comrades.

2

I will plant companionship thick as trees along all the rivers
    of America, and along the shores of the great lakes, and
    all over the prairies;
I will make inseparable cities, with their arms about each
    other's necks;
    By the love of comrades,
      By the manly love of comrades.

3

For you these, from me, O Democracy, to serve you, ma
    femme!
For you! for you, I am trilling these songs,
    In the love of comrades,
      In the high-towering love of comrades.

*   *   *   *

  When wealth is lost, nothing is lost;
  When health is lost, something is lost;
  When character is lost, all is lost!
  Motto Over the Walls of a School in Germany.

BE HAPPY . . . BE BETTER

GIVE us, O give us, the man who sings at his work! Be his occupation what it may, he is equal to any of those who follow the same pursuit in silent sullenness. He will do more in the same time—he will do it better—he will persevere longer.

THOMAS CARLYLE

All hearts grow warmer in the presence
Of one who, seeking not his own,
Gave freely for the love of giving,
Nor reaped for self the harvest sown.
Thy greeting smile was pledge and prelude
Of generous deeds and kindly words;
In thy large heart were fair guest-chambers,
Open to sunrise and the birds.

JOHN GREENLEAF WHITTIER

It is our daily duty to consider that in all circumstances of life, pleasurable, painful, or otherwise, the conduct of every human being affects, more or less, the happiness of others, especially of those in the same house; and that, as life is made up, for the most part, not of great occasions, but of small everyday moments, it is the giving to those moments their greatest amount of peace, pleasantness, and security, that contributes most to the sum of human good. Be peaceable. Be cheerful. Be true.—LEIGH HUNT.

WHAT IS MATURITY?
A STATEMENT OF UNUSUAL CLARITY
BY EDWARD A. STRECKER

MATURITY IS a quality of personality made up of a number of elements. It is stick-to-itiveness, the ability to stick to a job, to work on it and to struggle through it until it is finished, or until one has given all one has in the endeavor. It is the quality or capacity of giving more than is asked or required in a given situation. It is this characteristic that enables others to count on one; thus it is reliability. Persistence is an aspect of maturity; persistence to carry out a goal in the face of difficulties. Endurance enters into the concept of maturity; the endurance of difficulties, unpleasantness, discomfort, frustration, hardship.

The ability to size things up, make one's own decisions, is a characteristic of maturity. This implies a considerable amount of independence. A mature person is not dependent unless ill. Maturity includes a determination, a will to succeed and achieve, a will to live.

Of course, maturity represents the capacity to cooperate; to work with others; to work in an organization and under authority. The mature person is flexible, can defer to time, persons, circumstances. He can show tolerance. He can be patient and, above all, he has qualities of adaptability and compromise. Basically, maturity represents a wholesome amalgamation of two things: 1) Dissatisfaction with the status quo, which calls forth aggressive, constructive effort, and 2) Social concern and devotion. Emotional maturity is the morale of the individual."

"Every fault of the mind becomes more conspicuous and more guilty in proportion to the rank of the offender"— Persons in high station are not only answerable for their own conduct, but for the example they may hold out to others. This, joined to their advantages of education, aggravates their vices and loads them with a greater share of responsibility.

JUVENAL

Aim Your Life

by JENKIN LLOYD JONES

I SLEPT and dreamed that life was Beauty;
I woke and found that life was Duty.
Was thy dream then a shadowy lie?
Toil on, poor heart unceasingly;
And thou shalt find thy dream to be
A truth and noonday light to thee.

ELLEN STURGIS HOOPER

Man's heart is like a millstone, for ever swiftly at work, grinding its grist of thought and feeling and purpose. And, like a millstone, the heart will grind itself if it has nothing else to grind. So many men and women long for a life lifted above the need of work, a paradise of idleness! But there is nothing that keeps us so hale and sound, and in such full possession of our strength and the joy of living, as a steady round of duty, and solid work that we must dispose of, and for which we fill fit. God pity the vacant lives!

The most pitiable life is the aimless life. Heaven help the man or woman, the boy or girl, who is not interested in anything outside of his or her own immediate comfort and that related thereto; who eats bread to make strength for no special cause; who pursues science, reads poetry, studies books, for no earthly or heavenly purpose other than mere enjoyment or acquisition; who goes on accumulating wealth, piling up money, with no definite or absorbing purpose to apply it to anything in particular.

Not unless we fill our existence with an aim do we make it life.—REICHEL.

TIME: *MAKE USE OF IT*

Like the dew on the mountain,
   Like the foam on the river,
Like the bubble on the fountain
   Thou art gone, and forever!
         Sir Walter Scott—*Lady of the Lake*

Greatly begin! though thou have time
But for a line, be that sublime,—
Not failure, but low aim is crime.—J. R. Lowell.

By all means begin your folio; even if the doctor does not give you a year, even if he hesitates about a month, make one brave push and see what can be accomplished in a week. It is not only in finished undertakings that we ought to honour useful labour. A spirit goes out of the man who means execution, which outlives the most untimely ending. All who have meant good work with their whole hearts have done good work, although they may die before they have the time to sign it.—R. L. Stevenson.

It is better to busy one's-self about the smallest thing in the world than to treat a half-hour as worthless.—Goethe.

Iron rusts from disuse, stagnant water loses its purity and in cold weather becomes frozen; even so does inaction sap the vigors of the mind.—Leonardo da Vinci—1452-1519

FAITH LEADS TO SUCCESS

No one knows so well what a handicap can mean as the person who has lived with one. Raymond M. Dickinson, Superintendent Industrial Home and Services for the blind, Illinois Department of Public Welfare, lost useful vision as a result of an automobile accident in 1926, the year he graduated from high school. Yet, he went on to take a Ph.B. degree from the University of Chicago in 1930 majoring in philosophy and social science. He received Phi Beta Kappa honors.

Excerpts from an address given at the Regional Conference on Exceptional Children, held under the auspices of the Illinois Commission for Handicapped Children on May 5, 1958 at LaSalle, Illinois and printed in *Public Aid in Illinois*, December 1958.

No person ever lived on earth, save the Lord, himself, who was without handicaps. The writings of the ages, both literary and scientific, are full of stories of hardships, of human frailties and weaknesses, of the inroads of diseases and accidents, of triumphs over great and small problems. If this were not so, the history of mankind would be more placid and far less eventful than it is. Then too, human life would be a pretty dull period of existence.

*   *   *   *   *

My sphere of activity concerned with services to visually handicapped persons represents but a small fraction of this great field of social, educational, and community welfare. But it illustrates, I think, the basic principles involved. "We walk by faith, not by sight," says St. Paul, teaching the individual, handicapped or not, to see beyond his present circumstances to move forward to goals which he has set for himself, and to use his faith as driving-power to get where he wants to go.

Ideals and principles, then, are far more important than simply mechanical means, helpful as these are, and strong faith in them will overcome many obstacles. Some years ago a group of parents brought together to discuss and plan for the future of their blind children asked me to put in summary form a set of guiding ideals. After careful thought the following sonnet, which though specifically written for the blind, I think has general application, was the result. I have called it

CHALLENGE

What if I have eyes that do not see
This gaily colored world of forms and show;
What if in the dark I always go,
My footsteps led by sounds and memory;
What if autumn never dressed a tree
In golden brown for me to love and know;
And what if the sunset always hides its glow,
And morning's dawn does not unveil to me:
My father gave me strength of soul and mind;
My mother taught me how to laugh and pray;
My ears and nose and fingers are designed
To bring me knowledge, beauty, work, and play—
I do not envy those who see the light,
For I know my way and have no fear of night.

Faith means believing what is incredible, or it is no virtue at all. Hope means hoping when things are hopeless, or it is no virtue at all. And Charity means pardoning what is unpardonable, or it is no virtue at all.

– G. K. CHESTERTON, *Heretics*
LADIES HOME JOURNAL – February 1960

THE AMERICAN DREAM

Reprinted by permission of International Business Machines Corporation, from *Forces That Will Change America,* by Dr. Allan Nevins, THINK Magazine. Copyright 1959.

BENEATH the American faith in the future lie two main concepts, one material, the other at least potentially spiritual. The first is what James Truslow Adams called the American Dream. It is the hope of a better life than older lands and ages ever afforded: more security, more comfort, more money, wider horizons. No one should sneer at this concept just because it is necessarily material, for seekers of the American Dream performed prodigies of courage. Often they performed them unselfishly, thinking of their children rather than themselves. Willa Cather, looking at Nebraska, concluded that the earliest generation was truly heroic. "The generation that subdued the wild land and broke up the virgin prairies," she wrote, was an army of rugged men and women who "inspire respect and compel admiration." Their resourcefulness matched their courage. Beginning in the utter poverty of sod houses, they could look out at the end of their days on broad stretches of fertility and say, "We made this, with our backs and hands."

> *If only we are faithful to our past, we shall not have to fear our future. The cause of peace, justice and liberty need not fail and must not fail.*
>
> —JOHN FOSTER DULLES

SUCCESS?

He has achieved success who has lived well, laughed often, and loved much; who has gained the respect of intelligent men and the love of little children; who has filled his niche and accomplished his task; who has left the world better than he found it, whether by an improved poppy, a perfect poem, or a rescued soul; who has never lacked appreciation of earth's beauty or failed to express it; who has always looked for the best in others and given the best he had; whose life was an inspiration; whose memory a benediction.

If I can stop one heart from breaking,
I shall not live in vain;
If I can ease one life the aching,
Or cool one pain,
Or help one fainting robin
Unto his nest again,
I shall not live in vain;

—Emily Dickinson

In nothing do men more nearly approach the gods than in doing good to their fellow men.

—Cicero

The Turning Point in
My CAREER

by A. J. Cronin

From Readers Digest copyright 1941.

WHEN I was halfway through, the inevitable happened. A sudden desolation struck me like an avalanche. I asked myself: "Why am I wearing myself out with this toil for which I am so preposterously ill-equipped? What is the use of it? I ought to be resting ... conserving, not squandering my energies on this fantastic task." I threw down my pen. Feverishly, I read over the first chapters which had just arrived in typescript from my secretary in London. I was appalled. Never, never had I seen such nonsense in all my life. No one would read it. I saw, finally, that I was a presumptious lunatic, that all that I had written, all that I could ever write was wasted effort, sheer futility. I decided to abandon the whole thing. Abruptly, furiously, I bundled up the manuscript, went out, and threw it in the ash can.

Drawing a sullen satisfaction from my surrender, or, as I preferred to phrase it, my return to sanity, I went for a walk in the drizzling rain. Halfway down the loch shore I came upon old Angus, the farmer, patiently and laboriously ditching a patch of the bogged and peaty heath which made up the bulk of his hard-won little croft. As I drew near, he gazed up at me in some surprise: he knew of my intention and, with that inborn Scottish reverence for "letters," had tacitly approved it. When I told him what I had just done, and why, his weathered face slowly changed, his keen blue eyes, beneath misted sandy brows, scanned me with disappointment and a queer contempt. He was a silent man and it was long before he spoke. Even then his words were cryptic.

"No doubt you're the one that's right, doctor, and I'm the one that's wrong..." He seemed to look right to the bottom of me. "My father ditched this bog all his days and never made a pasture. I've dug it all *my* days and I've never made a pasture. But pasture or no pasture," he placed his foot dourly on the spade, "I canna help but dig. For my father knew and I know that if you only dig enough a pasture can be made here."

I understood. I watched his dogged working figure, with rising anger and resentment. I was resentful because he had what I had not: a terrible stubbornness to see the job through at all costs, an unquenchable flame of resolution brought to the simplest, the most arid duties of life. And suddenly my trivial dilemma became magnified, transmuted, until it stood as a touchstone of all human conduct. It became the timeless problem of mortality—the comfortable retreat, or the arduous advance without prospect of reward.

I trampled back to the farm, drenched, shamed, furious, and picked the soggy bundle from the ash can. I dried it in the kitchen oven. Then I flung it on the table and set to work again with a kind of frantic desperation. I lost myself in the ferociousness of my purpose. I would not be beaten, I would not give in. I wrote harder than ever. At last, toward the end of the third month, I wrote *finis*. The relief, the sense of emancipation, was unbelievable. I had kept my word. I had created a book. Whether it was good, bad or indifferent I did not care.

I chose a publisher by the simple expedient of closing my eyes and pricking a catalogue with a pin. I dispatched the completed manuscript and promptly forgot about it.

In the days which followed I gradually regained my health, and I began to chafe at idleness. I wanted to be back in harness.

At last the date of my deliverance drew near. I went round the village saying good-bye to the simple folk who had become my friends. As I entered the post office, the postmaster presented me with a telegram—an urgent invitation to meet the publisher. I took it straight away and showed it, without a word, to John Angus.

The novel I had thrown away was chosen by the Book Society, dramatized and serialized, translated into nineteen languages, bought by Hollywood. It has sold, to date, some three million copies. It has altered my life radically, beyond my wildest dreams . . . and all because of a timely lesson in the grace of perseverance.

But that lesson goes deeper still. Today, when the air resounds with shrill defeatist cries, when half of our stricken world is wailing in discouragement: "What is the use . . . to work . . . to save . . . to go on living . . . with Armageddon round the corner?" I am glad to recollect it. In this present chaos, with no shining vision to sustain us, the door is wide open to darkness and despair. The way to close that door is to stick to the job that we are doing, no matter how insignificant that job may be, to go on doing it, and to finish it.

Ignatius of Loyola was once playing a game of ball with his fellow students when someone demanded, suddenly and with due solemnity, what each of them would do if he knew he had to die in twenty minutes. All agreed that they would rush frantically to church and pray . . . all but Ignatius, who answered: "I should finish my game."

The virtue of all achievement, as known to Ignatius and my old Scots farmer, is victor over oneself. Those who know this victory can never know defeat.

The book A. J. Cronin threw away, then reclaimed and rewrote, was *Hatter's Castle*. It earned a fortune and made him famous. But far more important, it brought him the greatest triumph anyone can achieve—victory over himself. He went on to produce *The Citadel, The Keys of the Kingdom*, and many other popular books. But nothing gave him the intense satisfaction of that first great success: his conquest over doubt and despair.

SUCCESSFUL AGING

by MARTIN GUMPERT, M.D.

Taken from an article entitled OLD AGE AND PRODUCTIVE LOSS, appearing in Public Aid in Illinois, June 1954. The late Dr. Gumpert was a geriatrician of international repute as well as an accomplished author. Books for the general reader written by him include THE ANATOMY OF HAPPINESS and YOU ARE YOUNGER THAN YOU THINK.

I HAVE studied, recently, a considerable number of persons of far advanced age. I did not have a well-organized apparatus for research; I just talked to old people, deliberately not using any tests or schemes. I concentrated in this project on men and women who have succeeded in maintaining creative and productive activities in their various fields of endeavor, and are still full and valuable participants in life. Their average age was 80; the oldest was 92, the youngest 76. All are pioneers of successful aging. They represent *in nuce* the best our present civilization has been able to produce, and though they are of entirely different character, experience and standing, my aim was to discover common traits which would explain the successful management of their lives and might be of use to the common type of old person who spends his last years in misery and deterioration, afflicted by all the indignities of physical and social degradation.

The group investigated was comprised of statesmen, philosophers, scientists, artists, writers and businessmen, each one highly authoritative in his field, all able to enlarge their reputations and all still at work in an unbroken line of effort and skill and interest. All were of over-average intelligence and knowledge. Many had suffered hardships, and had fought violent battles on the bloody battlegrounds of our time. They certainly had not led what one would call a hygienic existence according to doctor's orders. Most had been exposed to stress or tragedy and had had to bear an unusual load of responsibilities. However, none had been, or is now, exposed to excessive wealth or poverty.

Age is a tyrant who forbids at the penalty of life all the pleasures of youth.

— MAXIM 461, LA ROCHEFOUCOULD

To start with my most primitive impressions: all were nice people whom I thoroughly enjoyed; all were still social forces who stimulated my mind and fed my intellectual curiosity. Some of them, whose lives and deeds are well-known, would have antagonized me exceedingly in their earlier years. Even by looking at their pictures, taken 30 or 40 years ago, past vanities, hostilities and tensions can be observed. All this has disappeared under the snow of old age. An old age of substance means growth in beauty and harmony. The flabby fat of adulthood dwindles, the eyes rule the face, wrinkles tell their story and are marks of un-mistakable identity in contrast to the mask we wear during our busy and ambitious years. The bony structure sharpens the profile and makes the genuine structure of these human beings transparent, and, finally, there is no need and no desire to restrain the emotions. From hardened, toughened fighters, these old persons have changed into soft, tender, warm human beings—often in moving contrast to the rigid-ity of their muscles and joints. There is no pompousness, but a melancholic sense of humor; there is shyness, and an animalic urge for contact; there is a reassuring sense of dig-nity and charm; and there is never fear of death.

Looking at them with a hard diagnostic eye, one might find nothing but an accumulation of symptoms of regression —but if such is regression, then my thesis is proved that in human beings, loss may take the character of productive gain.

Yet Time, who changes all, had altered him in soul and aspect as in age: years steal.
Fire from the mind as vigor from the limb; and life's enchanted cup but sparkles near the brim.

— *Child Harold*, LORD BYRON

"this above all
to thine own self be true"

HAMLET, ACT I, SCENE III—WILLIAM SHAKESPEARE

There, my blessing with thee!
And these few precepts in thy memory
See thou character. Give thy thoughts no tongue,
Nor any unproportion'd thought his act.
Be thou familiar, but by no means vulgar;
Those friends thou hast, and their adoption tried,
Grapple them to thy soul with hoops of steel;
But do not dull thy palm with entertainment
Of each new-hatch'd, unfledg'd comrade. Beware
Of entrance to a quarrel: but being in,
Bear't that the opposed may beware of thee.
Give every man thy ear, but few thy voice:
Take each man's censure, but reserve thy judgment.
Costly thy habit as thy purse can buy,
But not express'd in fancy: rich, not gaudy;
For the apparel oft proclaims the man.
And they in France of the best rank and station
Are most select and generous, chief in that.
Neither a borrower nor a lender be;
For loan oft loses both itself and friend,
And borrowing dulls the edge of husbandry.
This above all: to thine own self be true;
And it must follow, as the night the day,
Thou canst not then be false to any man.

*Truth is a gem that is found at a great depth; whilst
on the surface of this world, all things are weighed
by the false scale of custom.*

LORD BYRON

THE NATURE OF PERSECUTION

by

RALPH WALDO EMERSON

Born in Boston, 1803, graduated at Harvard, 1821, was a Unitarian clergyman, 1829-1832. In 1833, he began a career as lecturer and author, which continued for forty years. One of America's most celebrated essayists.

THE HISTORY of persecution is a history of endeavours to cheat nature, to make water run up hill, to twist a rope of sand. It makes no difference whether the actors be many or one, a tyrant or a mob. A mob is a society of bodies voluntarily bereaving themselves of reason, and traversing its work. The mob is man voluntarily descending to the nature of the beast. Its fit hour of activity is night. Its actions are insane like its whole constitution. It persecutes a principle; it would whip a right; it would tar and feather justice, by inflicting fire and outrage upon the houses and persons of those who have these. It resembles the prank of boys, who run with fire-engines to put out the ruddy aurora streaming to the stars. The inviolate spirit turns their spite against the wrongdoers. The martyr cannot be dishonoured. Every lash inflicted is a tongue of fame; every prison, a more illustrious abode; every burned book or house enlightens the world; every suppressed or expunged word reverberates through the earth from side to side.

"Ignorance," says a distinguished writer, "is the mother of superstition, of bigotry, of fanaticism, of disaffection, of cruelty, and of rebellion. These are its legitimate children. It never yet produced any other, and never will to the end of the world. And we may lay this down as an incontestable truth, that a well informed and intelligent people, more particularly a people well acquainted with the sacred writings, will always be more orderly, more decent, more humane, more virtuous, more religious, more obedient to their superiors, than a people totally devoid of all instruction and all education."

"TO EACH HIS OWN"

Taken From the Third Edition
in the Original Spelling

LET US ENJOY ACCORDING TO TASTE

From An Essay Concerning Humane Understanding
by JOHN LOCKE *published* 1690

A celebrated English philosopher, one of the most influential thinkers of modern times. He drew up (1669) the constitution for the colonists of Carolina.

§. 55. The Mind has a different relish, as well as the Palate; and you will as fruitlessly endeavour to delight all Men with Riches or Glory, (which yet some Men place their Happiness in,) as you would to satisfie all Men's Hunger with Cheese or Lobsters; which though very agreeable and delicious fare to some, are to others extremely nauseous and offensive: And many People would with Reason preferr the griping of an hungry Belly, to those Dishes, which are a Feast to others. Hence it was, I think, that the Philosophers of old did in vain enquire, whether *Summum bonum* (the chief good) consisted in Riches, or bodily Delights, or Virtue, or Contemplation: And they might have as reasonably disputed, whether the best Relish were to be found in Apples, Plumbs, or Nuts; and have divided themselves into Sects upon it. For as pleasant Tastes depend not on the things

*He labors vainly, who endeavors to
please every person.* —LATIN PROVERB

themselves, but their agreeableness to this or that particular Palate, wherein there is great variety: So the greatest Happiness consists, in the having those things which produce the greatest Pleasure, and the absence of those which cause any disturbance, any pain, which to different Men are very different things. If therefore Men in this Life only have hope; if in this Life they can only enjoy, 'tis not strange, nor unreasonable, they should seek their Happiness by avoiding all things that disease them here, and by preferring all that delight them; wherein it will be no wonder to find variety and difference. For if there be no Prospect beyond the Grave, the inference is certainly right, *Let us eat and drink,* let us enjoy what we delight in, *for to morrow we shall die.* This, I think, may serve to shew us the Reason, why, though all Men's desires tend to Happiness, yet they are not moved by the same Object. Men may chuse different things, and yet all chuse right, supposing them only like a Company of poor Insects, whereof some are Bees, delighted with Flowers, and their sweetness; others, Bettles, delighted with other kind of Viands; which having enjoyed for a Season, they should cease to be, and exist no more for ever.

> Now who shall arbitrate?
> Ten men love what I hate,
> Shun what I follow, slight what I receive;
> Ten, who in ears and eyes
> Match me: we all surmise,
> They, this thing, and I, that: whom
>   shall my soul believe?
>
> — Rabbi Ben Ezra, Robert Browning

HABIT IS THE FLYWHEEL
OF SOCIETY

by WILLIAM JAMES

"How perfectly replete is God's mind with all the laws and types of beauty. . . . The stately grace and majesty of the earth – its woods and plains, its streams and seas, the sunshine flashing over all, the sunsets gorgeous in their pomp of pillared amethyst, opal, gold. He pours the beauty of the moonlight, even upon a resting world, weird and fantastic, yet lovely as a dream. He spreads the infinite canopy of the night, and touches it everywhere with dots of splendor. He makes each season a moving panorama of sights and sounds, of brilliant gleams or fragrant odors, full, constantly, of beauty to him who studies it."

Habit is the enormous fly-wheel of society, its most precious conservation agent . . . There is no more miserable human being than one in whom nothing is habitual but indecision. Full half of the time of such a man goes to the deciding, or the regretting, of matters which ought to be so ingrained in him as practically not to exist for his consciousness at all.

That God rules in the affairs of men is as certain as any truth of physical science.

"LIFE'S UNDRESS REHEARSAL"
by HARRIET BEECHER STOWE

"TAKE us the foxes, the little foxes, that spoil the vines: for our vines have tender grapes."..."Little Foxes," by which I mean those unsuspected, unwatched, insignificant *little* causes that nibble away domestic happiness, and make home less than so noble an institution should be. You may build beautiful, convenient, attractive houses—you may hang the walls with lovely pictures and stud them with gems of Art; and there may be living there together persons bound by blood and affection in one common interest, leading a life common to themselves and apart from others; and these persons may each of them be possessed of good and noble traits; there may be a common basis of affection, of generosity, of good principle, of religion; and yet, through the influence of some of these perverse, nibbling, insignificant little foxes, half the clusters of happiness on these so promising vines may fail to come to maturity. A little community of people, all of whom may be willing to die for each other, may not be able to live happily together; that is, they may have far less happiness than their circumstances, their fine and excellent traits, entitle them to expect.

The reason for this in general is that home is a place not only of strong affections, but of entire unreserve; it is life's undress rehearsal, its back-room, its dressing-room, from which we go forth to more careful and guarded intercourse, leaving behind us much *débris* of cast-off and everyday clothing.

To be happy at home is the ultimate result of all ambition; the end to which every enterprise and labor tends, and of which every desire prompts the prosecution.

—JOHNSON

The First Quality of Success—
Get to the Point!

O NE of the striking characteristics of successful persons is their faculty of determining the relative importance of different things. There are many things which it is desirable to do, a few are essential, and there is no more useful quality of the human mind than that which enables its possessor at once to distinguish which the few essential things are. Life is so short and time so fleeting that much which one would wish to do must fain be omitted. He is fortunate who perceives at a glance what it will do, and what it will not do, to omit. This invaluable faculty, if not possessed in a remarkable degree naturally, is susceptible of cultivation to a considerable extent. Let any one adopt the practice of reflecting, every morning, what must necessarily be done during the day, and then begin by doing the most important things first, leaving the others to take their chance of being done or left undone. In this way attention first to the things of first importance soon acquires the almost irresistible force of habit, and becomes a rule of life. There is no rule more indispensable to success.

Procrastination is the thief of time.
                    —EDWARD YOUNG—*Night Thoughts*

. . . The greatest part of what we do or say being unnecessary, if a man takes this away he will have more leisure and less uneasiness. Accordingly, on every occasion a man should ask himself: "Is this one of the unnecessary things?" Now a man should take away not only unnecessary acts, but also unnecessary thoughts, for thus superfluous acts will not follow after.
                    —MARCUS AURELIUS

AVOID DECEPTION

BY WORD OR SILENCE

by JOHN RUSKIN

AND THIS is especially to be insisted on in the early education of young people. It should be pointed out to them with continual earnestness that the essence of lying is in deception, not in words: a lie may be told by silence, by equivocation, by the accent on a syllable, by a glance of the eye attaching a peculiar significance to a sentence; and all these kinds of lies are worse and baser by many degrees than a lie plainly worded; so that no form of blinded conscience is so far sunk as that which comforts itself for having deceived, because the deception was by gesture or silence, instead of utterance; and, finally, according to Tennyson's deep and trenchant line, "A lie which is half a truth is ever the worst of lies."

The age of our fathers, which was worse than that of our ancestors, produced us, who are about to raise a progeny even more vicious than ourselves.

HORACE

IN 1953, The Florentine Fior di Virtu, "Flowers of Virtue," was translated into English by Nicholas Fersin and published for the Library of Congress. The original copy from which the illustrations are taken and the translation made, was printed in Florence, Italy, in 1491, a year that marked the beginning of the decline of the golden era of art and learning in that great city of culture. Through the generous gift of Lessing J. Rosenwald, this priceless volume, along with others in his collection, belongs to the Library of Congress.

The text of the Fior is a collection gathered from many sources including the Holy Fathers, the Bible, early philosophers and others. There are 41 chapters in the book which "treats of all human vices which should be avoided by the man who wants to live according to God, and it teaches how one must acquire virtues and righteous customs according to the authority of holy theologians and many outstanding philosophers."

For some of the basic human traits, these next few pages give the admonitions found in this treasury of advice that dates back nearly 500 years.

THE VIRTUE OF COURAGE
"HE WHO IS BRAVE IS FREE"

FORTITUDE, according to Macrobius, can be of three kinds. First to be naturally strong of body. But this is not a virtue. Second is courage, or audacity of character, fearlessness in all grave and adverse things. Third is patience, enabling us patiently to endure all adversity and all distress. The last two are truly fortitude and are real virtues.

We may compare the virtue of fortitude to the lion. He always sleeps with his eyes open and when hunters come after him, he immediately begins sweeping his footsteps with his tail so as not to betray himself by leaving traces. But when he sees that he cannot escape, he comes against the hunters without any fear, valiantly engaging them in battle. Cicero says of the virtue called fortitude: "Man must be brave in battle and patient in adversity." Seneca says: "He who is brave is free." Lucius says: "Man is loved mainly because of two virtues: courage first, loyalty second." Socrates says: "It takes more courage to flee when necessary than to die." Brother Egidius says that courage may be of many kinds. One is to be brave before the danger of death when nothing else can be done. This is forced courage. Another is to be brave and bold out of habit of combat. A third is to be brave because of the company one keeps. Still another is to be valiant when one's opponent is weak and cowardly. Fifth is to be so bold that one does not fear anything. This is not fortitude but animal fury. These five kinds of fortitude are not perfect. The sixth kind is perfect and constitutes a virtue: that is when a man desires to be brave and persevering in order to avoid dishonor and any shortcoming within his soul or his body or his property. Or to be brave for one's faith, or for one's country.

If all the world were just, there would be no need of valour.
—PLUTARCH

HUMILITY

"He Who Humbles Himself Will Be Exalted"

ACCORDING to Origines, humility consists of curbing one's loftiness of spirit and one's vain desires. But this repression must not reach the point where one falls into the vice of dejection. St. Andronicus says that it is not good to humble oneself excessively and that dejection is a vice. Note that humility can be of many kinds. Showing oneself to be smaller than others. Being graciously submissive. Believing that one is not complete in all ways. Fearing all those things that should be feared. From humility stem the following virtues: the first one is obeisance, that is paying esteem to others. The second is reverence, that is to revere those greater than oneself. The third is obedience, meaning to obey those who have the right to command. The fourth is gratitude, or the deserving and the recognizing any service or benefaction received.

We may compare the virtue of humility to the lamb who is the mildest animal in the world. He endures all that is done to him and submits to everybody's will. That is why in the Holy Scriptures he is compared to the Son of God with the saying: Lamb of God who Takes the Sins of the World upon Thyself. Of this virtue Solomon says: "If anyone should give thee power over all his belongings, do not exalt thyself but rather act so as to make him appear master

Wisdom is ofttimes nearer when we stop than when we soar.
— THE EXCURSION, HENRY WADSWORTH

of all thy things." Jesus, son of Sirach, says: "Do not ask
for things that are loftier than thou." And he also says:
"The greater man thou art, the more thou shouldst be humble in every way in this life. Then in the other life, before
God, thou wilst be welcome." Jesus Christ says: "He who
humbles himself will be exalted, and he who exalts himself
will be humbled." St. Peter says: "God resists and opposes
proud people, but he gives His grace to the humble." St.
Jerome says: "One reaches the height of virtue not through
greatness, but through humility." Aristotle says: "If you
really want to know a man, give him power. The evil man
will become proud, but the good man will become more
humble than he was before." Longinus says: "Just as the
birds draw in their wings when they want to fly higher, thus
we should restrict and humble the man who wants to reach
high status." Aristotle says: "Honor others, for honor belongs to the one who bestows it and not to the one who
receives it." Seneca says: "Never praise anyone in their
presence." Socrates says: "No honor is ever lost, for if the
one to whom you have given it does not return it, then
someone else will give it to you instead." Solomon says,
speaking of the virtue of reverence: "Humble thy soul before God, and thy head before the great rulers, and lower
your ears to hear the cries of the poor." Cato says: "Step
aside before thy betters." Jesus, son of Sirach, says: "Son,
thou shalt acquire grace from God and from the world by
being reverent and respectful." St. Isidore says: "Do not
try to become equal to thy betters and do not despise neither
great nor humble."

Humility is a virtue all preach, none practise; and yet everybody is content to hear.　　　　— TABLE TALK, JOHN SELDEN

ON THE NATURE
OF
FRIENDSHIP

THE third love, called friendship or companionship, consists of wanting permissible and honest things from one another, just as Cicero tells us in his book "On Friendship." Such friendship has its foundation in a righteous and charitable unification of the aims of life when two persons enjoy talking and living and being one with the other. Such a love comes from three sources. The first is when a man only desires and hopes to obtain some advantage from his friend. Such a friendship, or love, is a false love and cannot justly be called either friendship or love, but rather a mercenary striving for gain, as is well expressed by Cicero in his book "On the Nature of God." The second is when a man wishes well for his friend without thinking of his own welfare. And this is perfect love. The third is when one wants to share with the other, and this is good friendship and good love. The test of this true and good love lies in three main things. The first is to love one's friend with a pure heart and to do what one thinks will bring him pleasure. The second is to avoid doing what one thinks will displease him or will be detrimental to him. Friends are made and kept three ways. First, by honoring them in their presence. Second, by saying good of them in their absence. Third, by serving them in their needs. On this subject Solomon says: "Nothing can be compared to a faithful friend." Ovid says: "You will find many friends in prosperity. But in adversity you will find yourself alone." Four things are better old than new: wine, fish, oil, but above all an old friend. Aristotle says: "The older the tree the more it needs support." And similarly, the older the man the more need he has of a friend, for there can be no good when one is alone. In the opinion of certain moral philosophers happiness is nothing but love and friendship for others. This is true if we speak of the moral happiness in

A friend to everybody is a friend to nobody.
—SPANISH PROVERB

this life and do not refer to the eternal happiness which is naught except God. This is what Cicero wanted to say in his book "On Friendship" when he quoted the saying of that great master Archita of Tarentino who said that if a man were to go to heaven and were to behold the beauty of the sun and of the moon and of the stars and all the other beauties of heaven and of earth and of the whole universe, and then were to return to earth—all this joy would be nothing for him unless he had someone to whom he could relate it and with whom he could discuss it as though with himself. It would even be a bitter grief for him. Plato and Seneca both say: "Before loving someone, test him. And having tested him, love him with good heart." And note also: a good man is corrupted by bad company, while a bad man becomes righteous in good company and rids himself of his infamy by keeping company with one better than himself.

He loved me well;
so well he could but die
To show he loved me better
than his life; he lost it
for me.
— JOHN DRYDEN

There are few subjects which have been more written upon, and less understood, than that of friendship. To follow the dictates of some, this virtue, instead of being the assuager of pain, becomes the source of every inconvenience. Such speculatists, by expecting too much from friendship, dissolve the connection, and by drawing the bands too closely, at length break them.
— OLIVER GOLDSMITH

LOYALTY

"BE LOYAL TO THOSE WHO TRUST YOU"

LOYALTY, according to Terence, is pure and perfect faith, never showing one thing for another.

The virtue of loyalty may be compared to the cranes. They have a king and they all serve him with more loyalty than is encountered in any other animal. At night, when they go to sleep, they place their king in the middle and they surround him and they always send two or three among them to stand guard. And these, in order not to fall asleep, keep a foot up in the air, while the other stands on the ground. And in the foot which is up they always hold a stone so that, should sleep surprise them, the stone would fall and they would feel it. And this they do out of loyalty to one another to protect their king and the other cranes who sleep. Seneca says: "He who loses faith cannot lose anything else." Solomon says: "Many people are called pious, but you will not find many who are loyal."

Socrates says: "Be loyal to those who trust you and you are certain never to have a bad end." Juvenal says: "Everything on earth is praised by somebody, criticized by somebody else—but loyalty and truthfulness are praised by all." Longinus says: "There are three ways whereby a man may become great: being loyal, telling the truth and not thinking idle thoughts."

I like a Highland friend who will stand by me, not only when I am in the right, but when I am a little in the wrong.

—SIR WALTER SCOTT

JOY

*The grand essentials to happiness in this life are
something to do, something to love, and something to hope for.*
— JOSEPH ADDISON

ACCORDING to Priscianus joy, a consequence of love,
is spiritual rest and contentment and enjoyment of any
pleasure. Jesus, son of Sirach, says that the life of man consists of heartfelt joy, although it is a vice and not a virtue to
enjoy those things which are not proper. St. Augustine says
that sudden sadness always follows worldly joy.

We may compare the virtue of joyfulness to the rooster
who sings day and night according to the hours, moved by
the natural cheerfulness in his heart and who arranges his
joyous life reasonably and in orderly fashion. Solomon says:
"There is no wealth greater than the health of the body,
there is no joy greater than the joy of the heart." And he
also says: "A cheerful heart causes man's life to blossom,
while the spirit of sadness dries the bones. Never rejoice at
other people's misfortunes, for you cannot know when adversity may come to you." Seneca says: "In prosperity do not
rejoice too much and in adversity be not downcast."

*The supreme happiness of life is the conviction of being loved
for yourself, or, more correctly, being loved in spite of yourself.*
— VICTOR HUGO

ENVY

"THERE IS NO GREATER TORMENT"

ENVY, WHICH is the vice opposite to the virtue of love, may be of two kinds. The first is when we are saddened by the fortune of others, whereas the second is when we exult at the misfortunes of others. But both these feelings may at times exist without any vice. For it is good to exult at other people's defects in order that they may correct them, and to despise their good fortune in order to keep them from becoming arrogant. But before we can have full understanding of such a feeling, we must well see and understand the nature of virtue itself. Aristotle says that virtue is a good quality of one's mind whereby one lives righteously and avoids evil. And virtue is also an ordered, well built mind. It is not a natural or artificial physical beauty, but rather resides in the soul, in reason, in piety of life and customs, in love of God and in honor.

We may compare the vice of envy to the magpie who is a bird so envious that when she sees her young getting fat in the nest, she hits them in the ribs with her beak so as to infect their flesh and make them thin. Seneca says that envy draws evil from good and good from evil. And he also says that it is easier to avoid distress at poverty than envy of riches. And we read in the "Summa" of vices that just as the worm gnaws wood and vermin eats up clothes, so envy corrodes man. Solomon says: "When your enemy falls and is ruined, do not rejoice at his ruin, for it does not please God." And also: "He who rejoices at other people's misfortunes will not go unpunished." St. Gregory says that

> The most certain sign of being born with great qualities is to be born without envy.
> —LA ROCHEFOUCAULD

there is no greater torment in the world than envy and that where there is envy there cannot be love. The greatest vengeance one may invent against an envious man is to do him good. Seneca says: "Do not offend anyone and do not acquire enemies. But envy does both to a high degree." Ovid says: "Envy always makes grass seem higher in other people's meadows." Plato says: "An envious man is never free of pain, just as the hypocrite is never free from fear." St. Augustine says: "He who is envious can love no one, and so there can be no worse vice than envy." Homer says: "One should fear the envy of relatives and friends more than the envy of enemies." Ptolemy says: "The envious man is even content to suffer loss in order to damage someone else."

About this vice of envy we read in the Old Testament. Cain saw that his brother Abel was prospering and that from day to day all his property was improving. This happened because he received these graces from God. Out of envy Cain slew his brother with a club. And Cain and Abel were the first two brothers that ever lived on earth and this was the first blood ever shed in the world.

Envy is blind, and she has no other quality than that of detracting from virtue. —LIVY

Emulation looks out for merits, that she
may exalt herself by victory;
Envy spies out blemishes, that she may
lower another by defeat.

—CHARLES CALEB COLTON

HUMOR

Will Rogers—concerning his rope
spinning act said, "Spinnin' a rope
is fun, if your neck ain't in it."
—WILL ROGERS
Wit and Wisdom

And in that town a dog was found,
    As many dogs there be,
Both mongrel, puppy, whelp, and hound,
    And curs of low degree.
The dog, to gain his private ends,
    Went mad, and bit the man.

                *   *   *   *

The man recovered of the bite,
    The dog it was that died.
        GOLDSMITH. *Elegy on the Death of a Mad Dog.*

And the night shall be filled with music,
    And the cares that infest the day
Shall fold their tents like the Arabs,
    And as silently steal away.
    LONGFELLOW. *The Day is Done.*

Small debts are like small shot; they are rattling
on every side, and can scarcely be escaped without a
wound; great debts are like cannon; of loud noise,
but little danger.
    DR. JOHNSON. *Letter to Jos. Simpson, Esq.*

IF I SHOULD DIE

by BEN KING

IF I should die to-night
And you should come to my cold corpse and say,
Weeping and heartsick o'er my lifeless clay—
If I should die tonight,
And you should come in deepest grief and woe—
And say: "There's that ten dollars that I owe,"
I might arise in my large white cravat
And say, "What's that?"

If I should die to-night
And you should come to my cold corpse and kneel,
Clasping my bier to show the grief you feel,
I say, if I should die to-night
And you should come to me, and there and then
Just even hint 'bout payin' me that ten,
I might arise the while,
But I'd drop dead again.

THREE MEN ON THIRD

Reprinted by permission of Doubleday & Company, Inc., from *Three Men on Third,* by Ira L. Smith and H. Allen Smith. Copyright 1951.

THE day that Brooklyn accumulated three runners on third was August 15, 1926, when the Dodgers were engaging the Braves at Ebbetts Field. In case you don't remember it, here are the details:

Brooklyn came to bat in the seventh. Johnny Butler singled. DeBerry hit a two-bagger scoring Butler. Dazzy Vance singled and DeBerry went to third. Fewster was hit by the pitcher, filling the bases. Jacobson popped out. Babe Herman now took his place at the plate. The stage was all set for the drama. Herman belted a line drive to right field and DeBerry vacated third base and crossed the plate. Vance, who had been on second, thought Herman's drive was going to be caught, and held up until he was certain the outfielder had missed it; then Dazzy started for home. He rounded third, ran halfway to the plate, decided he wouldn't be able to beat the throw-in, reversed himself and started back to third. Meanwhile Fewster was tearing around the base paths from first, arriving at the third sack about the time Vance returned to it. They stood and looked at each other in astonishment for a few moments and then switched their attention to an even more astonishing sight. Babe Herman figured he had a double, possibly a triple, and he preferred a triple of course, and was bent on trying to stretch it. He had his head down and was running for all he was worth, with no suspicion in his mind that a traffic jam had already developed at third. He didn't raise his head until he was a few feet from third and then when he looked up, there stood Vance and Fewster, and the Boston third baseman was just taking the throw. This third baseman, Taylor, was understandably excited. He received the throw and started tagging people. He tagged every human being within reach, including the third base umpire. Herman, however, had got himself out of range and was heading back for second. Taylor fired the ball down to the shortstop and Herman was tagged out before he could reach the bag.

That episode became a sort of baseball classic, possibly because the unpredictable Babe Herman was involved in the making of it. Bennett Cerf has told the story of the time a few years later, when Quentin Reynolds was sitting in the last row of seats in the grandstand at Ebbetts Field during the early innings of an important game. Chancing to look into the street outside the park, Reynolds saw a latecomer, a Brooklyn fan who was running along the pavement, puffing heavily as he headed for the entrance.

"Better hurry up!" Reynolds yelled down to the man. "You're missing something big. The Dodgers have three men on base."

"Yehr?" cried the fan. "Which base?"

> When earth's last ball game is finished,
> And the crowd has passed from the stand,
> When the youngest fan has subsided
> And gone to the Promised Land
> We shall rest—and gosh!—we shall need it,
> Knock off for a season or two,
> Till the greatest of all the Series
> Shall set us to root anew.

—from Walter Pulitzer's parody on Kipling's *L'Envoi* as appearing in My 66 Years in the Big Leagues by Connie Mack. John C. Winston Company

THE GROUCH

MY DEAR FELLOW-GRUMBLERS: Poets, philosophers, and fools, in all ages, have been writing and preaching on the art of being happy, without a mighty sight of *seals* to their ministry, I guess.

But, as many can't be satisfied unless *miserable* in body and mind, I am going to show all such persons the several means to be used for the attainment of such a desirable end.

In the first place, my beloved whiners, in order to attain an end, you must get up a stiff resolution and determination to *conquer*. Yes, my hearers, you must set down your foot, grit your teeth, let your resolution be as stiff as boilerplate, let your firmness be as unwavering as the rocks of Gibraltar. Be determined to be miserable, and you shall get your desires. Never mind what people tell you about the bounties of Providence and the beauties of Nature, the balmy breezes of spring, the twittering and warbling of birds,—you must sheer off from them like a wealthy upstart from a poor relation.

Put on a sour, savage, snapping-turtle physiognomy; look daggers, and *act out* your feelings; this is the first great commandment with misery: Think you are the most forsaken mortal that misery ever held a mortgage on. *Hate* mankind; call 'em all liars, cheats, swindlers, villains. Look at everything on the wrong side. If it has no dark side, *make* one, just so as to enjoy yourself looking at it. Take it for granted that everybody about is especially interested to torment you. Fight everybody and everything. You can't hit amiss. The world is all *wrong*. Everybody is a villain but *yourself*, and it is your duty to teach mankind manners. Go at 'em. You can't *fail* to be miserable.

THE JACK POT SHOT

THIS guy was huntin' and the gun he used was one of these muzzle loaders — you have to put your powder in, then your wad in, and then your shot. All right. He had plenty of powder, and he only had enough lead to load one time. So he looked and he could see a turkey settin' up on a limb. So he loaded his gun with this last load; then he looked back — beneath the limb stood a deer. Heard a racket down under his feet — was a rattlesnake. So he was setting' near a stream and he finally decided to shoot the turkey and take chances on the rattlesnake bitin'. So he was kinda nervous when he drew his gun. He shot a little too low. Part of his load went into the turkey, the other part went in the limb. The limb fell on the deer and killed him, ramrod fell out of his gun killed the rattlesnake. The gun kicked him backwards into the stream and when he came up he had his shirt tail full of fish. So he carried home deer, turkey, and fish.

> *He was a mighty hunter before the Lord;*
> *Wherefore it is said, even as Nimrod the*
> *mighty hunter before the Lord.*
>
> *—Genesis* **X,** 9

WILL ROGERS was born in Oologah, Indian Territory, November 4, 1879, and died in a plane crash with Wiley Post near Point Barrow, Alaska, in 1935. His homely philosophy, unfailing humor and keen observation, as exemplified in these comments, have made him an American institution.

Papers today say, "what would Lincoln do today?" Well, in the first place he wouldn't chop any wood, he would trade his ax in on a Ford. Being a Republican he would vote the Democratic ticket. Being in sympathy for the under dog he would be classed as a radical Progressive. Having a sense of humor he would be called eccentric.

It's great to be great but it's greater to be human.

One revolution is just like one cocktail, it just gets you organized for the next.

Half our life is spent trying to find something to do with the time we have rushed through life trying to save.

We know lots of things we didn't use to know but we don't know any way to prevent 'em happening.

Our investigations have always contributed more to our amusement than they have to knowledge.

A conservative is a man who has plenty of money and don't see any reason why he shouldn't always have plenty of money.

A difference of opinion is what makes horse racing and missionaries.

A holding company is like a fellow handing the other fellow the swag while they search you.

There ain't nothing that breaks up homes, country and nations like somebody publishing their memoirs.

"He won by two lengths going away"

BROADWAY BOSWELL

From
The Damon Runyon Story by ED WEINER
LONGMANS, GREEN AND CO., N. Y., COPYRIGHT 1948

DAMON WAS in Louisville, Kentucky, on May 17, 1940, when Earle Sande, the jockey, brought in Gallant Fox to win the Kentucky Derby. In the press box there was the usual excitement when the horse raced across the finish line. Then the reporters settled back in their seats, attempting to compose themselves, struggling for the leads of their stories. Damon showed no emotion. He stood near his typewriter, lighted a cigarette, and remembered. Sande had been his favorite jockey since 1922 when he first saw him bring in a winner for Harry Sinclair. He was then wearing the white silks of the Rancocas Stable. In 1924, when Sande was badly hurt in a spill at Saratoga and announced he would never ride again, Damon regarded it as one of the sporting tragedies of the year. He wrote a poem that began:

> Maybe there'll be another,
>   Heady an' game, an' true—
> Maybe they'll find his brother
>   At drivin' them horses through.
>
> Maybe—but, say, I doubt it.
>   Never his like again—
> Never a handy
> Guy like Sande
>   Bootin' them babies in!

And now, sixteen years later, Damon was watching him win again. He sat down, placed his cigarette on a table near his typewriter, and began writing. Most of the other reporters have forgotten the stories they wrote that day, but they still remember Damon's lead. It is probably the most famous piece of verse he ever wrote.

Say, have they turned the pages
    Back to the past once more?
Back to the racin' ages
    An' a Derby out of the yore?
Say, don't tell me I'm daffy,
    Ain't that the same ol' grin?
Why it's that handy
Guy named Sande,
Bootin' a winner in!

Say, don't tell me I'm batty!
    Say, don't tell me I'm blind!
Look at that seat so natty!
    Look how he drives from behind!
Gone is the white of the Ranco,
    An' the white band under his chin—
Still he's that handy
Guy named Sande,
Bootin' a winner in!

Maybe he ain't no chicken,
    Maybe he's gettin' along,
But the ol' heart's still a-tickin'
    An' the old bean's goin' strong.
Roll back the year! Yea, roll 'em!
    Say, but I'm young agin,
Watchin' that handy
Guy named Sande,
Bootin' a winner in!

Then Damon began his account of the race.
"Why, it wasn't even close!
"Gallant Fox, pride of the East, with the old master mind
of the horsemen sitting in his saddle as easily as if he were
in a rocking chair on a shady veranda, galloped off with
the $50,000 Kentucky Derby this afternoon. He won by
two lengths, going away."

Experience join'd with common sense,
To mortals is a providence.
                    —JOHN RICHARD GREEN

WHAT THE GOVERNOR
OF MASSACHUSETTS SAID
TO THE GOVERNOR OF MAINE

From IT'S A LONG TIME BETWEEN DRINKS
by JAMES N. TIDWELL *in Western Folklore*

WHETHER they drink or not, most Americans know that the Governor of North Carolina once remarked to the Governor of South Carolina, "It's a long time between drinks." But the circumstances under which that remark was first made are unknown. An early version of the origin occurs in *Puck* on March 5, 1879:

But we are reminded that once the Governor of North Carolina, after feasting the Governor of South Carolina; and having been told by the Governor of S. C. that the same would be reciprocated, telegraphed: "It's a long time between drinks."

The phrase must have been widely known even in 1879; otherwise *Puck* could not have published the following on June 4:

Q. What did the Governor of Massachusetts say to the Governor of Maine?

Ans. There's too much drinking between times.

*The first draught a man drinks ought to be for thirst,
the second for nourishment, the third for pleasure,
the fourth for madness.*

*They never taste who always drink;
They always talk who never think.*

— MATTHEW PRIOR

How to Tell a Story

by

MARK TWAIN

I DO NOT CLAIM that I can tell a story as it ought to be told. I only claim to know how a story ought to be told, for I have been almost daily in the company of the most expert story-tellers for many years.

There are several kinds of stories, but only one difficult kind—the humorous. I will talk mainly about that one. The humorous story is American, the comic story is English, the witty story is French. The humorous story depends for its effect upon the *manner* of the telling; the comic story and the witty story upon the *matter*.

The humorous story may be spun out to great length, and may wander around as much as it pleases, and arrive nowhere in particular; but the comic and witty stories must be brief and end with a point. The humorous story bubbles gently along, the others burst.

The humorous story is strictly a work of art – high and delicate art – and only an artist can tell it; but no art is necessary in telling the comic and the witty story; anybody can do it. The art of telling a humorous story—understand, I mean by word of mouth, not print—was created in America, and has remained at home.

The humorous story is told gravely; the teller does his best to conceal the fact that he even dimly suspects that there is anything funny about it; but the teller of the comic story tells you beforehand that it is one of the funniest things he has ever heard, then tells it with eager delight, and is the first person to laugh when he gets through. And sometimes, if he has had good success, he is so glad and happy that he will repeat the "nub" of it and glance around from face to face, collecting applause, and then repeat it again. It is a pathetic thing to see.

Very often, of course, the rambling and disjointed humorous story finishes with a nub, point, snapper, or whatever you like to call it. Then the listener must be alert, for in many cases the teller will divert attention from that nub by dropping it in a carefully casual and indifferent way, with the pretence that he does not know it is a nub.

Artemus Ward used that trick a good deal; then when the belated audience presently caught the joke he would look up with innocent surprise, as if wondering what they had found to laugh at. Dan Setchell used it before him. Nye and Riley and others use it today.

But the teller of the comic story does not slur the nub; he shouts it at you—every time. And when he prints it, in England, France, Germany, and Italy, he italicizes it, puts some whooping exclamation-points after it, and sometimes explains it in a parenthesis. All of which is very depressing, and makes one want to renounce joking and lead a better life.

A jest's prosperity lies in the ear
Of him that hears it, never in the tongue
Of him who makes it.
—Love's Labour Lost, WILLIAM SHAKESPEARE

A man's reputation is what his friends say about him. His character is what his enemies say about him.

To string incongruities and absurdities together in a wandering and sometimes purposeless way, and seem innocently unaware that they are absurdities, is the basis of the American art, if my position is correct. Another feature is the slurring of the point. A third is the dropping of a studied remark apparently without knowing it, as if one were thinking aloud. The fourth and last is the pause.

Artemus Ward dealt in numbers three and four a good deal. He would begin to tell with great animation something which he seemed to think was wonderful; then lose confidence, and after an apparently absent-minded pause add an incongruous remark in a soliloquizing way; and that was the remark intended to explode the mine — and it did.

For instance, he would say eagerly, excitedly, "I once knew a man in New Zealand who hadn't a tooth in his head" —here his animation would die out; a silent, reflective pause would follow, then he would say dreamily, and as if to himself, "and yet that man could beat a drum better than any man I ever saw."

The pause is an exceedingly important feature in any kind of story, and a frequently recurring feature, too. It is a dainty thing, and delicate, and also uncertain and treacherous; for it must be exactly the right length—no more and no less—or it fails of its purpose and makes trouble. If the pause is too short the impressive point is passed, and the audience have had time to divine that a surprise is intended—and then you can't surprise them, of course.

Mingle a little folly with your wisdom; a little nonsense now and then is pleasant.

CARMINA HORACE

A friend is a fellow who knows all about you and still likes you.

HIT WITHOUT A WORRY

by Arthur Daley

W ILLIE MAYS drilled a ball through the left side of the infield the other day and he had his 3,000th hit as a big leaguer. Thus did he reach another plateau of the many he has scaled during his spectacular career. But this had extra significance because he joined one of baseball's more exclusive clubs, one with a membership of only 10.

Willie ranks high on all lists of signal accomplishment and he will keep advancing on all of them for as long as he is able to continue operations, a time limit that is fuzzy and ill-defined. After all, the 'Mazing Mays is thirty-nine years old and isn't quite what he used to be.

But two important goals lie ahead, one in the distant future and the other slightly more immediate. Five years after Willie sheds his Giant uniform for the last time he will be elected to the Hall of Fame at Cooperstown. It could be and should be unanimous. But before that happens his home run total will have approached the seemingly unapproachable career record of 714 set by Babe Ruth.

Willie came into this season with 600 homers, the first man other than the Babe to reach that figure. A year ago he had dismissed from his mind even a mild notion of ever impinging on such sacred territory. Now he is more hesitant, almost as if he harbors a flicker of hope.

A bow to Henry

"If I can get 35 homers this year," he said the other day, groping for words that came with uncertainty, "and if I can then jump off to a good start next spring...." His voice trailed off and he stared into space before adding, "I can get close to 700. I don't expect to but it isn't an impossibility. I don't worry about records."

This was a switch from the fellow who had stated flatly a year earlier, "I ain't got a chance of catching the Babe.

He was in a class by himself." But Willie won't be too far behind when he calls it quits. He was quick to offer another challenger, though.

"Henry Aaron has a better chance than I have," he said. "He's a couple of years younger and should be up near 600 by the end of this season. Besides, he's in a better home run park. That's why I think he has a shot at it."

As Willie approached his 3,000th hit he was totally unconcerned. He showed none of the strains that had weighed him down as he approached three of his home run milestones. The first heavy pressure period came just before he hit his 512th homer to pass Mel Ott as the Giant kingpin. The second came before he smote his 535th to go ahead of Jimmy Foxx and become baseball's premier right-handed homer monarch. The third travail was when he strove for No. 600.

"I'm not worrying about my 3,000th hit," he said a few days before he attained it. "I know I'll get it because there are so many ways a man can make a hit. Homers are different. That's when you feel the pressure."

I was one of the lucky ones who was at the Polo Grounds when Willie made his first hit and his first homer. They came in the same package; a titanic blast off Warren Spahn sent the ball bouncing off the left-field roof and Willie was on his way. It was such a joy to watch Mays in the exuberance of his extreme youth. Few ballplayers supplied such memorable moments.

They still rave about his catch of the monstrous drive by Vic Wertz against the deep center-field wall in the 1954 World Series. But I have a different favorite. It came in a game against the Dodgers in Willie's freshman season, the year historians refer to as the Little Miracle of Coogan's Bluff when Bobby Thomson's last-inning home run in the final play-off game won the pennant for the Giants.

Dazzling double play

Earlier that year the transpontine rivals met at the Polo Grounds. The score was tied in the ninth and Brooklyn had runners on first and third with one out. Carl Furillo lashed a line drive to right center and Billy Cox, the fast runner on third, properly tagged up. Willie raced across the gap and speared the ball with outstretched glove.

The run had to score after the catch, it seemed, because there was no way that Willie could brake to a halt, set himself and throw in time because he was facing in the wrong direction. But no one should ever underestimate Willie's baseball instincts, even as an unexperienced kid of twenty.

He just spun counterclockwise. What he had to do was unorthodox, but Willie knew it was the only way. He came out of his spin throwing the ball to the plate. It didn't even bounce. It was a strike to Wes Westrum and Cox was ten feet down the line to be tagged out in a fantastic double play.

"That was the most perfectest throw I ever made," said Willie.

"He'll have to do it again before I'll believe it," said a stunned Charlie Dressen, the Dodger manager. But that's why Willie has worn the mantle of greatness for so long. He has always been doing the unbelievable.

The Fisherman's Song

From

THE COMPLEAT ANGLER

by Izaak Walton

Oh the brave Fishers life,
It is the best of any,
'Tis full of pleasure, void of strife,
And 'tis belov'd of many:
  Other joyes
  are but toyes,
  only this
  lawful is,
  for our skil
  breeds no ill,
but content and pleasure.
In a morning up we rise
Ere Aurora's peeping,
Drink a cup to wash our eyes,
Leave the sluggard sleeping:
  Then we go
  too and fro,
  with our knacks
  at our backs,
  to such streams
  as the Thames
if we have the leisure.
When we please to walk abroad
For our recreation,
In the fields is our abode,
Full of delectation:
  Where in a Brook
  with a hook,
  or a Lake
  fish we take,
  there we sit
  for a bit,
till we fish intangle.

We have Gentles in a horn,
We have Paste and worms too,
We can watch both night and morn,
Suffer rain and storms too;
    None do here
    use to swear,
    oathes do fray
    fish away,
    we sit still,
    watch our quill,
Fishers must not rangle.

If the Sun's excessive heat
Makes our bodies swelter
To an Osier hedge we get
For a friendly shelter,
    where in a dike
    Pearch or Pike,
    Roch or Dace
    we do chase
    Bleak or Gudgion
    without grudging,
we are still contented.

Or we sometime pass an hour,
Under a green willow,
That defends us from a showr,
Making earth our pillow,
    There we may
    think and pray
    before death
    stops our breath;
    other joyes
    are but toyes
and to be lamented.

From his dark haunt beneath the tangled roots
Of pendent trees, the Monarch of the brook,
Behooves you then to ply your finest art.

The Seasons, **JAMES THOMSON**

BILLS OF FARE

to Tempt Your Palate and

Tickle Your Ribs

From *The Berkshire News Comic Cook Book and Dispeptics Guide to the Grave*, by Fred H. Curtiss. Copyright 1890 by Douglas Brothers, Publishers, Great Barrington, Massachusetts. Reprinted from *Treasury of American Folk Humor* by James M. Tidwell, Crown Publishers, Inc., N. Y.

SOME tact should be observed in arranging a *menu*. They are generally written in French; this one therefore is prepared in United States:

Oysters or eggs on the half shell.

Bean Soup.

Shad.   Sauce from the cook.

Sliced cucumbers and Jamaica Ginger.

Colt steaks.   Sheepshead sauce.

Roast beef, plenty of gravy.

Tired eggs, turned over.

Hens, stuffed with soldier buttons.

Tame cheese.

Ice cream garnished with green peas.

Apples and Peanuts.

Sage Tea.

Here's another in French:

MENU.

Huitres, 6 per quartre.

Potage au taisez vous.

Saumon aux no bones.

Ris de veaux.   Sauce, new mown hay.

Ris de Daible.   Sauce nixey.

Fillet de bœuf red hot.

Punch *a la* John L.

It was a common saying among the Puritans, "Brown bread and the Gospel is good fare."

—Commentaries, Isaiah, MATTHEW HENRY

FROM "THE CELEBRATED JUMPING FROG OF CALAVERAS COUNTY"

A purportedly true occurrence in the mining camps of California in the spring of 1849 that duplicates in basic facts a story entitled The Athenian and the Frog *that is reported in classic Greek as having occurred two thousand years ago. From* The Man That Corrupted Hadleyburg *by* MARK TWAIN, Harper & Brothers Publishers.

Well, thish-yer Smiley had rat-tarriers and chicken cocks, and tom-cats, and all of them kind of things, till you couldn't rest, and you couldn't fetch nothing for him to bet on but he'd match you. He ketched a frog one day, and took him home, and said he cal'lated to educate him; and so he never done nothing for three months but set in his back yard and learn that frog to jump. And you bet you he *did* learn him, too. He'd give him a little punch behind, and the next minute you'd see that frog whirling in the air like a doughnut—see him turn one summerset, or maybe a couple if he got a good start, and come down flat-footed and all right, like a cat. He got him up so in the matter of ketching flies, and kep' him in practice so constant, that he'd nail a fly every time as fur as he could see him. Smiley said all a frog wanted was education, and he could do 'most anything – and I believe him. Why, I've seen him set Dan'l Webster down here on this floor—Dan'l Webster was the name of the frog—and sing out, "Flies, Dan'l, flies!" and quicker'n you could wink he'd spring straight up and snake a fly off'n the counter there, and flop down on the floor ag'in as solid as a gob of mud, and fall to scratching the side of his head with his hind foot as indifferent as if he hadn't no idea he'd been doin' any more'n any frog might do. You never see a frog so modest and straightfor'ard as he was, for all he was so gifted. And when it come to fair and square jumping on a dead level, he could get over more ground at one straddle than any animal of his breed you ever see. Jumping on a dead level was his strong suit, you understand; and when it came to that, Smiley would ante up money on him as long as he had a red. Smiley was monstrous proud of his frog, and well he might be, for fellers that had travelled and been everywheres all said he laid over any frog that ever *they* see.

Well, Smiley kep' the beast in a little lattice box, and he used to fetch him down-town sometimes and lay for a bet. One day a feller – a stranger in the camp, he was – come acrost him with his box, and says:

"What might it be that you've got in the box?"

And Smiley says, sorter indifferent-like, "It might be a parrot, or it might be a canary, maybe, but it ain't – it's only just a frog."

And the feller took it, and looked at it careful, and turned it round this way and that, and says, "H'm – so 'tis. Well, what's *he* good for?"

"Well," Smiley says, easy and careless, "he's good enough for *one* thing, I should judge – he can outjump any frog in Calaveras County."

The feller took the box again and took another long, particular look, and give it back to Smiley, and says, very deliberate: "Well," he says, "I don't see no p'ints about that frog that's any better'n any other frog."

"Maybe you don't," Smiley says. "Maybe you understand frogs and maybe you don't understand 'em; maybe you've had experience, and maybe you ain't only a amature, as it were. Anyways, I've got *my* opinion, and I'll resk forty dollars that he can outjump any frog in Calaveras County."

And the feller studies a minute, and then says, kinder sad like, "Well, I'm only a stranger here, and I ain't got no frog, but if I had a frog I'd bet you."

And then Smiley says: "That's all right—that's all right; if you'll hold my box a minute, I'll go and get you a frog." And so the feller took the box and put up his forty dollars along with Smiley's and set down to wait.

So he set there a good while thinking and thinking to hisself, and then he got the frog out and prized his mouth open and took a teaspoon and filled him full of quail shot—

Bets at the first were fool-traps, where the wise
Like spiders lay in ambush for the flies.

JOHN DRYDEN

filled him pretty near up to his chin—and set him on the floor. Smiley he went to the swamp and slopped around in the mud for a long time, and finally he ketched a frog and fetched him in and give him to this feller, and says:

"Now, if you're ready, set him alongside of Dan'l, with his fore-paws just even with Dan'l's, and I'll give the word." Then he says, "One—two—three—*git!*" and him and the feller touched up the frogs from behind, and the new frog hopped off lively; but Dan'l give a heave, and hysted up his shoulders—so—like a Frenchman, but it warn't no use—he couldn't budge; he was planted as solid as a church, and he couldn't no more stir than if he was anchored out. Smiley was a good deal surprised, and he was disgusted, too, but he didn't have no idea what the matter was, of course.

The feller took the money and started away; and when he was going out at the door he sorter perked his thumb over his shoulder—so—at Dan'l, and says again, very deliberate: "Well," he says, "*I* don't see no p'ints about that frog that's any better'n any other frog."

Smiley he stood scratching his head and looking down at Dan'l a long time, and at last he says, "I do wonder what in the nation that frog throwed off for—I wonder if there ain't something the matter with him—he 'pears to look mighty baggy, somehow." And he ketched Dan'l by the nape of the neck, and hefted him, and says, "Why blame my cats if he don't weigh five pounds!" and turned him upsidedown, and he belched out a double handful of shot. And then he see how it was, and he was the maddest man—he set the frog down and took out after that feller, but he never ketched him.

Some play for gain; to pass time others play
For nothing; both play the fool, I say:
Nor time nor coin I'll lose, or idly spend;
Who gets by play, proves loser in the end.

"ALL SINNERS GO OUT"

Reprinted by courtesy of Crown Publishers, Inc., TREASURY OF AMERICAN FOLK HUMOR, from *Flashes and Sparks of Wit and Humor by Our American Humorists.*

When Mr. Moody was on a journey, in the western part of Massachusetts, he called on a brother in the ministry on Saturday, to spend the Sabbath with him. He offered to preach, but his friend objected on account of his congregation having got into a habit of going out before the meeting was closed. "If that is all, I must and will stop and preach for you," was Moody's reply. When Mr. Moody had opened the meeting and named his text, he looked around on the assembly and said: "My hearers, I am going to speak to two sorts of folks today—saints and sinners! Sinners! I am going to give you your portion first, and would have you give good attention." When he had preached to them as long as he thought best, he paused and said, "There, sinners, I have done with you now; you may take your hats and go out of the meeting-house as soon as you please." But all tarried and heard him through.

BRIBERY BACKFIRES

From *American Wit and Humor*, George W. Jacobs & Co.

"IT'S $100 in your pocket," whispered the defendant's lawyer to the juror, "if you can bring in a verdict of manslaughter in the second degree." Such proved to be the verdict, and the lawyer thanked the juror warmly as he paid him the money. "Yes," said the juror, "it was tough work, but I got there after a while. All the rest went in for acquittal."

Who thinketh to buy villainy with gold,
Shall ever find such faith so bought—so sold.
— WILLIAM SHAKESPEARE

DOUBLE TALK

Reprinted by courtesy of Crown Publishers, Inc., from TREASURY OF AMERICAN FOLK HUMOR, by James M. Tidwell, from *American Wit and Humor*. George W. Jacobs & Co., Philadelphia.

"OUR paper is two days late this week," writes a Nebraska editor, "owing to an accident to our press. When we started to run the press Wednesday night, as usual, one of the guy ropes gave away, allowing the forward glider fluke to fall and break as it struck the flunker flopper. This, of course, as any one who knows anything about a press will readily understand, left the gang-plank with only the flip flap to support it, which also dropped and broke off the wooper-chock. This loosened the fluking from between the ranrod and the flipper-snatcher, which also caused trouble. The report that the delay was caused by the over-indulgence in stimulants by ourselves, is a tissue of falsehoods, the peeled appearance of our right eye being caused by our going into the hatchway of the press in our anxiety to start it, and pulling the coupling pin after the slap-bang was broken, which caused the dingus to rise up and welt us in the optic. We expect a brand-new glider fluke on this afternoon's train."

> 'Twas brillig, and the slithy toves
>   Did gyre and gimble in the wabe;
> All mimsy were the borogoves,
>   And the mome raths outgrabe.

> "Beware the Jabberwock, my son!
>   The jaws that bite, the claws that catch!
> Beware the Jubjub bird, and shun
>   The frumious Bandersnatch!"
>   —The Hunting of the Snark, LEWIS CARROLL

Common Consent

Reprinted by courtesy of Crown Publishers, Inc., from TREAS-
URY OF AMERICAN FOLK HUMOR, by James M. Tidwell,
from *Folk Laughter on the American Frontier,* by Mody C. Boatright. The Macmillan Co., New York, 1949.

...ONE day a wagon with several occupants drew up in front of the county courthouse. A young man got out and came into the office of the county clerk.

"Is this the place where a feller comes to git a license to git married?" he asked.

"Yes, sir," answered the clerk. "You surely have come to the right place."

"Well, make me out a license so that John Brown can marry Samathy Smith."

"Are you John Brown?"

"Yes, I'm John Brown."

"And is the young lady of age?"

"Naw she ain't."

"Then I suppose you have her father's permission to marry her?"

"Well, I guess I have. See that old man a-settin' out there in that wagon with a shotgun across his lap? Well, that's her father."

"Have you a criminal lawyer in this burg?"

"We think so but we haven't been able to prove it on him."

A little nonsense now and then
Is relished by the wisest men.

JUST AN OVERSIGHT

From "Now I'll Tell One"

By Harry Hirshfield

Copyright Chilton Company, 1938

SMITH, Jones and Greene came to the big city to attend the Horseradish Dealers' Convention. They got a room together on the sixtieth floor of a hotel. That night they went out for a bit of excitement and returned about 2 A.M. As they entered the lobby of the hotel, the clerk informed the trio that the elevators had broken down and would not be fixed until morning. He would arrange cots for them in the lobby.

"No, no," answered Jones. "We'll walk up."

"But you are on the sixtieth floor," reminded the clerk.

"We know it – but just the same, we'll walk up."

As the three started up the stairs, Jones again suggested something. "Boys, after all, it's sixty floors, so I have an idea. To keep it interesting while we walk up, for the first twenty floors I'll sing. The next twenty flights, Smith, you tell jokes – and, as you are by nature a sad guy, Greene, you'll tell sad stories for the last twenty floors. Anything to keep up the interest."

Up they started. Jones sang for twenty flights. Then up to the fortieth floor Smith told nifty jokes. As they started for the final twenty Jones said, "Now Greene, you tell sad stories."

"Have, I got something sad to tell you immediately," moaned Greene! "I forgot to take the keys."

When speculation has done its worst, two and two still make four. —Samuel Johnson

The Way Old Tige Barked

From *Folk Laughter on the American Frontier*
by MODY C. BOATRIGHT, p. 100-101
THE MACMILLAN CO., N. Y.

THERE was once a backwoodsman who boasted that his hound Tige was the best hunting dog in seven counties. He said that he never went hunting that Tige did not tree a varmint and that by the way he barked old Tige always told him what the varmint was.

A newcomer to the settlement, who thought that the old-timer must be stretching the blanket a bit, offered to bet that old Tige could not tell one varmint from another. So to settle the wager the men went hunting the next night. They turned Tige loose in the creek bottom and told him to sic.

"There ain't no use in walking around a lot," said the backwoodsman. "Old Tige will let us know when he finds something."

They had not been sitting long when old Tige was heard.

"Jest wait," said the settler. "He ain't treed yet."

They sat for a few minutes longer, then old Tige sounded a new note.

"He's treed now," said the backwoodsman.

"What's he got?" asked the newcomer.

"I reckon that must be a bobcat."

When they reached the tree and held up their torch, sure enough there was a bobcat. They shot it and put Tige on the trail again.

After a while Tige bayed.

"He's treed," said the old-timer.

"What's he got this time?"

"I reckon that must be a possum."

They came to the tree, and sure enough there was the possum.

Again they sat while Tige ranged and again Tige bayed.

"What's Tige got this time?"

It follows not, because
The hair is rough, the dog's a savage one.

The Daughter—SHERIDAN KNOWLES

"I reckon that must be a coon."

Again the prediction proved correct.

The newcomer was ready to pay the wager, but the night was young and old-timer was eager for more hunting. So Tige was put on the trail and presently he bayed again.

Then suddenly his bark changed to a long howl that seemed to shake the trees and hills.

"What's Tige got now?" asked the newcomer.

"Tige ain't got nothing," replied the backwoodsman, jumping to his feet. "Something's got Tige."

With eye upraised his master's looks to scan,
The joy, the solace, and the aid of man;
The rich man's guardian, and the poor man's friend,
The only creature faithful to the end.

*—*GEORGE CRABBE

The owl shriek'd at thy birth, an evil sign;
The night-crow cried, aboding luckless time;
Dogs howl'd, and hideous tempests shook down trees;
The raven rook'd her on the chimney's top,
And chattering pies in dismal discords sung.

*Henry VI, Act V—*WILLIAM SHAKESPEARE

Page Eighty Seven

SERIOUS POLITICS

Reprinted from *Stories and Speeches of William O. Bradley,* with biographical sketch by M. H. Thatcher. Copyright 1916 by Transylvania Printing Co., Lexington, Kentucky.

IN THE campaign of 1900 [Lieutenant Governor Bill] Thorne told the following story in a political speech:

It was just after W. O. Bradley was elected Governor of Kentucky, and the Republicans in my county were holding a big ratification meeting. Brass bands, all kinds of floats and banners, and hundreds of men, women and boys paraded the streets. A young girl claimed that while standing on her front porch, which was almost covered with vines and foliage of different kinds, she was repeatedly hugged and kissed by a young man she hardly knew. A warrant was sworn out for her assailant. He was arrested and it was my duty as Commonwealth's Attorney to prosecute him. John D. Carroll, now Judge of the Kentucky Court of Appeals, had been employed to defend him. I soon finished my examination of the witness and turned her over to Carroll for cross examination.

"What night was this?" thundered Carroll.

"Thursday night," answered the witness.

"Thursday night, you say? What time of night?"

"About eight o'clock."

"That was about the time the parade was passing your house?"

"Yes."

"Did you ever cry out or scream?"

"No, sir, I did not."

"Will you tell this jury," asked Carroll with rising voice, "with the streets thronged with people, and this man hugging and kissing you against your will, as you claim, why you never uttered a single cry for help or assistance?"

"Yes, sir. I will tell the jury, and everybody else, that you'll never ketch me hollerin' at no Republican gatherin'."

Bread Cast Upon the Waters . . .

A NUN was sitting at a window in her convent one day . . . when she was handed a letter from home. Upon opening it a ten-dollar bill dropped out. She was most pleased at receiving the gift from her home folks, but as she read the letter her attention was distracted by the actions of a shabbily dressed stranger who was leaning against a post in front of the convent.

She couldn't get him off her mind and, thinking that he might be in financial difficulties, she took the ten-dollar bill and wrapped it in a piece of paper, on which she had written, "Don't despair, Sister Eulalia," and threw it out of the window to him. He picked it up, read it, looked at her with a puzzled expression, tipped his hat and went off down the street.

The next day she was in her cell saying her beads when she was told that some man was at her door who insisted on seeing her. She went down and found the shabbily dressed stranger waiting for her. Without saying a word he handed her a roll of bills. When she asked what they were for he replied, "That's the sixty bucks you have coming. Don't Despair paid 5-1."

> *In play there are two pleasures for your choosing—*
> *The one is winning, and the other losing.*
>
> *—Don Juan,* LORD BYRON

Will Rogers' Advice to the Candidates

"GO FISHING UNTIL ELECTION"

by WILL ROGERS

There should be a moratorium called on candidates speeches. They have both called each other everything in the world they can think of. From now on they are just talking themselves out of votes. The high office of President of the United States has degenerated into two ordinarily fine men being goaded on by their political leeches into saying things that if they were in their right minds they wouldn't think of saying. Imagine Mr. Hoover last night "any change of policies will bring disaster to every fireside in America." Of all the conceit. This country is a thousand times bigger than any two men in it, or any two parties in it. These big politicians are so serious about themselves and their parties. This country has gotten where it is in spite of politics, not by the aid of it. That we have carried as much political bunk as we have and still survived shows we are a super nation. If by some divine act of Providence we could get rid of both these parties and hired some good man, like any other big business does, why that would be sitting pretty. This calamity was brought on by the actions of the people of the whole world and its weight will be lifted off by the actions of the people of the whole world, and not by a Republican or a Democrat. So you two boys just get the weight of the world off your shoulders and go fishing. Both of you claim you like to fish, now instead of calling each other names till next Tuesday, why you can do everybody a big favor by going fishing, and you will be surprised but the old U.S. will keep right on running while you boys are sitting on the bank. Then come back next Wednesday and we will let you know which one is the lesser of the two evils of you.

The difference between a politician and a statesman is that the politician thinks of the next election while the statesman thinks of the next generation.

CHIQUITA

by BRET HARTE

BEAUTIFUL! Sir, you may so. Thar isn't her match
in the county.
Is thar, old gal,—Chiquita, my darling, my beauty?
Feel of that neck, sir—thar's velvet! Whoa! steady—ah,
will you, you vixen!
Whoa! I say. Jack, trot her out; let the gentleman look
at her paces.

Morgan!—she ain't nothing else, and I've got the papers
to prove it.
Sired by Chippewa Chief, and twelve hundred dollars
won't buy her.
Briggs of Tuolumne owned her. Did you know Briggs
of Tuolumne?
Busted hisself in White Pine, and blew out his brains
down in Frisco?

Hedn't no savey, hed Briggs. Thar, Jack! that'll do,—
quit that foolin'!
Nothin' to what she kin do, when she's got her work cut
out before her.
Hosses is hosses, you know, and likewise, too, jockeys is
jockeys;
And 'tain't ev'ry man as can ride as knows what a hoss
has got in him.

Know the old ford on the Fork, that nearly got Flani-
gan's leaders?
Nasty in daylight, you bet, and a mighty rough ford in
low water!
Well, it ain't six weeks ago that me and the Jedge and
his nevey
Struck for that ford in the night, in the rain, and the
water all round us;

Up to our flanks in the gulch, and Rattlesnake Creek just
a-bilin',
Not a plank left in the dam, and nary a bridge on the
river.
I had the grey, and the Jedge has his roan, and his nevey,
Chiquita;
And after us trundled the rocks jest loosed from the top
of the cañon.

Lickity, lickity, switch, we came to the ford, and Chiquita
Buckled right down to her work, and, afore I could yell
to her rider,
Took water jest at the ford, and there was the Jedge and
me standing,
And twelve hundred dollars of hoss-flesh afloat, and
a-driftin' to thunder!

Would ye b'lieve it? That night that hoss, that 'ar filly,
Chiquita,
Walked herself into her stall, and stood there, all quiet
and dripping:
Clean as a beaver or rat, with nary a buckle of harness,
Just as she swam the Fork,—that hoss, that ar' filly,
Chiquita.

That's what I call a hoss! and – What did you say? – Oh,
the nevey?
Drownded, I reckon,—leastways, he never kem back to
deny it.
Ye see the derned fool had no seat; ye couldn't have made
him a rider;
And then, ye know, boys will be boys, and hosses – well
hosses is hosses!

Four things greater than all things are,—
Women and Horses and Power and War.
—RUDYARD KIPLING

BEN FRANKLIN

*I saw Few Die of Hunger . . . of eating
a hundred thousand.*
— BEN FRANKLIN
Poor Richard Almanac
1736

Who quick be to borrow, and slow be to
   pay,
Their credit is naught, go they never so
   gay.
   TUSSER. *Five Hundred Points of Good
   Husbandry. Good Husbandry Lessons.
   33.*

Talk of your science! after all is said
There's nothing like a bare and shiny
   head;
Age lends the graces that are sure to
   please;
Folks want their doctors mouldy, like
   their cheese.
   HOLMES. *Rip Van Winkle, M.D. Canto ii.*

ANNIVERSARY

*A very brief view of Benjamin Franklin's remarkable
career — 170 years after his death — with
some of his writing*

POSSIBLY the most celebrated American philosopher,
statesman, diplomat, and author, Benjamin Franklin, is
quoted more widely in the United States than almost any
other source of meaningful phrases. He was an intellectual
giant at a time of many great men. His versatile gifts have
seldom been equaled in history.

Born at the beginning of the 18th Century, at Boston,
on January 17, 1706, he traveled to Philadelphia, where
he spent most of his illustrious life. He learned the printer's
trade in the office of his elder brother, James, and in 1729,
established himself as an editor and proprietor of the *Pennsylvania Gazette.* He founded the Philadelphia library in
1731 and began the publication of *Poor Richard's Almanac*
in 1732. In 1743, he founded the University of Pennsylvania
and in 1752, he demonstrated, by experiments made with a
kite during a thunderstorm, that lightning is a discharge of
electricity. He was elected to the second Continental Congress in 1775, and in 1776 was a member of a committee of
five chosen by Congress to draw up a declaration of independence. He went to Paris in late 1776 as ambassador to the
court of France and helped conclude a treaty with France,
February 6, 1778, by which France recognized the independence of America. In 1783, he helped conclude the Treaty of
Paris with England.

He returned to America in 1785. He served as a delegate
to the constitutional convention in 1787. His long and brilliant career ended with his death at Philadelphia, April 17,
1790.

This very brief summary of an extremely full and productive life serves only to show how remarkable it was that
Franklin had any time for literary output. Yet, his writings
were voluminous and are still extremely quotable. In *The
Way to Wealth* and *Advice to Young Tradesmen,* you will
find more interesting phrases packed into a few pages than
in any other short article you have ever read.

BENJAMIN FRANKLIN TELLS
OF HIS INTEREST IN BOOKS

FROM a child I was fond of reading, and all the little money that came into my hands was ever laid out in books. Pleased with the Pilgrim's Progress, my first collection was of John Bunyan's works in separate little volumes. I afterward sold them to enable me to buy R. Burton's Historical Collections; they were small chapman's books, and cheap, 40 or 50 in all. My father's little library consisted chiefly of books in polemic divinity, most of which I read, and have since often regretted that, at a time when I had such a thirst for knowledge, more proper books had not fallen in my way, since it was now resolved I should not be a clergyman. Plutarch's Lives there was in which I read abundantly, and I still think that time spent to great advantage. There was also a book of De Foe's, called an Essay on Projects, and another of Dr. Mather's, called Essays to do Good, which perhaps gave me a turn of thinking that had an influence on some of the principal future events of my life.

This bookish inclination at length determined my father to make me a printer, though he had already one son (James) of that profession. In 1717 my brother James returned from England with a press and letters to set up his business in Boston. I liked it much better than that of my father, but still had a hankering for the sea. To prevent the apprehended effect of such an inclination, my father was impatient to have me bound to my brother. I stood out some time, but at last was persuaded, and signed the indentures when I was yet but twelve years old. I was to serve as an apprentice till I was twenty-one years of age, only I was to be allowed journeyman's wages during the last year. In a little time I made great proficiency in the business, and became a useful hand to my brother. I now had access to better

Books should to one of these four ends conduce
For wisdom, piety, delight or use.

Of Prudence, SIR JOHN DENHAM

books. An acquaintance with the apprentices of booksellers enabled me sometimes to borrow a small one, which I was careful to return soon and clean. Often I sat up in my room reading the greatest part of the night, when the book was borrowed in the evening and to be returned early in the morning, lest it should be missed or wanted.

And after some time an ingenious tradesman, Mr. Matthew Adams, who had a pretty collection of books, and who frequented our printing-house, took notice of me, invited me to his library, and very kindly lent me such books as I chose to read. I now took a fancy to poetry, and made some little pieces; my brother, thinking it might turn to account, encouraged me, and put me on composing occasional ballads. One was called *The Lighthouse Tragedy*, and contained an account of the drowning of Captain Worthilake, with his two daughters: the other was a sailor's song, on the taking of *Teach* (or Blackbeard) the pirate. They were wretched stuff, in the Grub-street-ballad style; and when they were printed he sent me about the town to sell them. The first sold wonderfully, the event being recent, having made a great noise. This flattered my vanity; but my father discouraged me by ridiculing my performances, and telling me versemakers were generally beggars.

Reading maketh a full man; conference a ready man; and writing an exact man.
—*On Studies*—SIR FRANCIS BACON

The welfare of America is closely bound up with the welfare of mankind. From Lafayette to his wife

THE
WAY
To
WEALTH
by DR. BENJAMIN FRANKLIN

He that by the Plough would thrive,
Himself must either hold or drive.

As published by Simeon Ide
Windsor, Vt.
1826

I HAVE heard, that nothing gives an author so great pleasure, as to find his works respectfully quoted by others. Judge, then, how much I must have been gratified by an incident I am going to relate to you. I stopped my horse, lately, where a great number of people were collected at an auction of merchant's goods. The hour of sale not being come, they were conversing on the badness of the times; and one of the company called to a plain, clean old man, with white locks, "Pray, father Abraham, what think you of the times? will not these heavy taxes quite ruin the country? How shall we be ever able to pay them? what would you advise us to?" Father Abraham stood up, and replied, "If you would have my advice, I will give it you in short; 'for a word to the wise is enough,' as Poor Richard says." They joined in desiring him to speak his mind, and gathering round him, he proceeded as follows:

"Friends, (says he) the taxes are, indeed, very heavy; and if those laid on by the government were the only ones we had to pay, we might more easily discharge them: but we have many others, and much more grievous to some of us. We are taxed twice as much by our idleness, three times as much by our pride, and four times as much by our folly; and from these taxes the commissioners cannot ease or deliver us, by allowing an abatement. However, let us hearken to good advice, and something may be done for us; "God helps them that help themselves," as Poor Richard says.

I. It would be thought a hard government that should tax its people one tenth part of their time, to be employed in its service: but idleness taxes many of us much more; sloth, by bringing on diseases, absolutely shortens life. "Sloth, like rust, consumes faster than labour wears, while the used key is always bright," as Poor Richard says. "But dost thou love life, then do not squander time, for that is the stuff life is made of," as Poor Richard says." How much more than is necessary do we spend in sleep? forgetting that "the sleeping fox catches no poultry, and that there will be sleeping enough in the grave," as Poor Richard says.

If time be of all things the most precious, wasting time must be, as Poor Richard says, "the greatest prodigality; since (as he elsewhere tells us) lost time is never found again, and what we call time enough, always proves little enough;" let us then up and be doing, and doing to the purpose; so by diligence shall we do more with less perplexity. "Sloth makes all things difficult, but industry all easy; and, he that riseth late must trot all day, and shall scarce overtake his business at night; while laziness travels so slowly that poverty soon overtakes him. Drive thy business, let not that drive thee; and early to bed and early to rise, makes a man healthy, wealthy and wise," as Poor Richard says.

So what signifies wishing and hoping for better times? We may make these times better if we bestir ourselves. "Industry need not wish, and he that lives upon hope will die fasting. There are no gains without pains; then help hands, for I have no lands," or if I have they are smartly taxed. "He that hath a trade, hath an estate; and he that hath a calling, hath an office of profit and honour," as Poor Richard says; but then the trade must be worked at, and the calling well followed, or neither the estate nor the office will enable us to pay our taxes. If we are industrious, we will

"Drive thy business, let not that drive thee."
"He that lives on hope will die fasting."

never starve; for "at the workman's house hunger looks in, but dares not enter." Nor will the bailiff or the constable enter, for "Industry pays debts, while despair increaseth them." What though you have found no treasure, nor has any rich relation left you a legacy, "diligence is the mother of good luck, and God gives all things to industry. Then plough deep, while sluggards sleep, and you shall have corn to sell and to keep." Work while it is called to-day, for you know not how much you may be hindered to-morrow. "One to-day is worth two to-morrows," as Poor Richard says; and farther, "Never leave that till to-morrow which you can do to-day." If you were a servant, would you not be ashamed that a good master should catch you idle? Are you then your own master? be ashamed to catch yourself idle, when there is so much to be done for yourself, your family, your relations and your country. Handle your tools without mittens; remember, that "The cat in gloves catches no mice," as Poor Richard says. It is true, there is much to be done, and perhaps, you are weak-handed; but stick to it steadily, and you will see great effect; for "Constant dropping wears away stones; and by diligence and patience the mouse ate into the cable; and little strokes fell great oaks."

Methinks I hear some of you say, "Must a man afford himself no leisure." I will tell thee my friend, what Poor Richard says; "Employ thy time well, if thou meanest to gain leisure; and, since thou are not sure of a minute, throw not away an hour." Leisure is time for doing something useful; this leisure the diligent man will obtain, but the lazy man never; for, "A life of leisure and a life of laziness are two things. Many, without labour, would live by their wits only, but they break for want of stock;" whereas industry gives comfort, and plenty, and respect. "Fly pleasures and they will follow you. The diligent spinner has a large shift; and now I have a sheep and a cow, every body bids me good-morrow."

II. But with our industry, we must likewise be steady, settled, and careful, and oversee our own affairs with our own eyes, and not trust too much to others; for, as Poor Richard says,

"I never saw an oft removed tree,
Nor yet an oft removed family,
That throve so well as those that settled be."

And again, "three removes is as bad as a fire;" and again, "Keep thy shop, and thy shop will keep thee;" and again, "If you would have your business done, go; if not, send." And again,

"He that by the plough would thrive,
Himself must either hold or drive."

And again, "The eye of a master will do more work than both his hands;" and again, "Want of care does us more damage than want of knowledge;" and again, "Not to oversee workmen, is to leave them your purse open." Trusting too much to others' care is the ruin of many; for "In the affairs of this world, men are saved, not by faith, but by the want of it;" but a man's own care is profitable; for, "If you would have a faithful servant, and one that you like, serve yourself. A little neglect may breed great mischief, for want of a nail the shoe was lost; for want of a shoe the horse was lost; for want of a horse the rider was lost," being overtaken and slain by the enemy; all for the want of a little care about a horse-shoe nail.

"A fat kitchen makes a lean will."
"Women and wine, game and deceit,
Make the wealth small, and the want great."

III. So much for industry, my friends, and attention to one's own business; but to these we must add frugality, if we would make our industry more certainly successful. A man may, if he knows not how to save as he gets, "keep his nose all his life to the grindstone, and dies not worth a groat at last. A fat kitchen makes a lean will;" and

"Many estates are spent in the getting,
Since women for tea forsake spinning and knitting,
And men for punch forsake hewing and splitting."

If you would be wealthy, think of saving as well as getting. The Indies have not made Spain rich, because her outgoes are greater than her incomes.

Away, then, with your expensive follies, and you will not have so much cause to complain, of hard times, heavy taxes, and chargeable families; for,

"Women and wine, game and deceit,
Make the wealth small, and the want great."

And farther, "What maintains one vice, would bring up two children." You may think, perhaps, that a little tea, or a little punch now and then, diet a little more costly, clothes a little finer, and a little entertainment now and then, can be no great matter; but remember, "Many a little makes a mickle." Beware of little expenses; "A small leak will sink a great ship," as Poor Richard says; and again, "Who dainties love, shall beggars prove:" and moreover, "Fools make feasts, and wise men eat them." Here you are all got together to this sale of fineries and nick-nacks. You call them goods; but if you do not take care, they will prove evils to some of you. You expect they will be sold cheap; and perhaps they may, for less than they cost; but if you have no occasion for them, they must be dear to you. Remember what Poor Richard says: "Buy what thou hast no need of, and ere long thou shalt sell thy necessaries." And again, "At a great pennyworth pause awhile:" he means, that perhaps the cheapness is apparent only, and not real; or the bargain, by straitening thee in thy business, may do thee more harm than good. For in another place he says, "Many have been ruined by buying good pennyworths." Again, "It is foolish to lay out money in a purchase of repentance;" and yet this folly is practised every day at auctions, for want of minding the Almanack. Many a one, for the sake of finery on the back, has gone with a hungry belly, and half starved their families; "Silks and Satins, scarlet and velvets, put out the kitchen fire," as Poor Richard says. These are not the necessaries of life; they can scarcely be called the conveniences; and yet only because they look pretty, how many want to have them? By these and other extravagances, the genteel are reduced to poverty, and forced to borrow of those whom they formerly despised, but who, through industry and frugality, have maintained their standing; in which case it appears plainly, that "A ploughman on his legs is higher than a gentleman on his knees," as poor Richard says. Perhaps they have had a small estate left them, which they knew not the getting of: they think "It is day, and will never be night;" that a little to be spent out of so much is not worth minding; "but always taking out of the meal-tub, and never putting in, soon comes to the bottom," as Poor Richard says; and then, "When the well is dry, they know the worth of water." But this they might have known before, if they had taken his advice. "If you would know the value of money, go and try to borrow some; for he that goes a borrowing, goes a sorrowing," as Poor Richard says; and, indeed, so does he that lends to such people, when he

"Pride that dines on vanity, sups on contempt."
"Pride breakfasted with Plenty, dined with Poverty and
supped with Infamy."

goes to get it again. Poor Dick further advises, and says,
  "Fond pride of dress is sure a very curse,
  Ere fancy you consult, consult your purse."
And again, "Pride is as loud a beggar as want, and a great
deal more saucy." When you have bought one fine thing,
you must buy ten more, that your appearance may be all
of a piece;" but Poor Dick says, "It is easier to suppress
the first desire, than to satisfy all that follow it; and it is
as truly folly for the poor to ape the rich, as for the frog
to swell, in order to equal the ox.
  "Vessels large may venture more,
  But little boats should keep near shore."
  It is, however, a folly soon punished; for, as Poor Richard
says; "Pride that dines on vanity, sups on contempt. Pride
breakfasted with Plenty, dined with Poverty, and supped
with Infamy." And, after all, of what use is this pride of
appearance for which so much is risked, so much suffered?
It cannot promote health, nor ease pain; it makes no increase of merit in the person; it creates envy, it hastens
misfortune.
  But what madness must it be, to run in debt for these
superfluities? We are offered by the terms of this sale, six
months credit, and that, perhaps, has induced some of us
to attend it, because we cannot spare the ready money, and
hope now to be fine without it. But ah! think what you do
when you run in debt, you give to another power over your
liberty. If you cannot pay at the time, you will be ashamed
to see your creditor, you will be in fear when you speak to
him; you will make poor, pitiful, sneaking excuses, and by
degrees come to loose your veracity, and sink into base
downright lying, for "The second vice is lying, the first is
running in debt," as poor Richard says, and again to the

same purpose, "Lying rides upon Debt's back;" whereas a free American ought not to be ashamed, nor afraid to see or speak to any man living. But poverty often deprives a man of all spirit and virtue. "It is hard for an empty bag to stand upright." What would you think of that nation or that government, who should issue an edict, forbidding you to dress like a gentleman or gentlewoman, on pain of imprisonment or servitude? Would you not say, that you were free, have a right to dress as you please, and that such an edict would be a breach of your privileges, and such a government tyrannical? And yet you are about to put yourself under that tyranny when you run in debt for such a dress! Your creditor has authority, at his pleasure, to deprive you of your liberty, by confining you in jail for life, or by selling you for a servant, if you should not be able to pay him. When you have got your bargain, you may perhaps think little of payment! but, as poor Richard says, "Creditors have better memories than debtors; creditors are a superstitious sect, great observers of set days and times." The day comes round before you are aware, and the demand is made before you are prepared to satisfy it; or, if you bear your debt in mind, the term, which at first seemed so long, will, as it lessens, appear extremely short. Time will seem to have added wings to his heels as well as his shoulders. "Those have a short Lent, who owe money to be paid at Easter." At present, perhaps, you may think yourselves in thriving circumstances, and that you can bear a little extravagance without injury, but

"For age and want save while you may,
No morning sun lasts a whole day."

Gain may be temporary and uncertain; but ever, while you live, expense is constant and uncertain; and, "It is easier to build two chimneys, than to keep one in fuel," as poor Richard says; so "Rather go to bed supperless, than rise in debt."

"For age and want save while you may
No morning sun lasts a whole day."

"Get what you can, and what you get hold,
'Tis the stone that will turn all your lead into gold."
And when you have got the philosopher's stone, sure you will no longer complain of bad times or the difficulty of paying taxes.

IV. This doctrine, my friends, is reason and wisdom: but after all, do not depend too much upon your own industry, frugality, and prudence, though excellent things, for they may all be blasted, without the blessing of Heaven, and therefore ask that blessing humbly, and be not uncharitable to those that at present seem to want it, but comfort and help them. Remember, Job suffered, and was afterwards prosperous.

And now to conclude, "Experience keeps a dear school, but fools will learn in no other," as Poor Richard says, and scarce in that; for it is true, "We may give advice but we cannot give conduct." However, remember this, "They that will not be counselled cannot be helped." And farther, that "If you will not hear Reason, she will surely rap your knuckles," as Poor Richard says."

Thus the old gentleman ended his harrangue. The people heard it, and approved the doctrine, and immediately practised the contrary, just as if it had been a common sermon; for the auction opened, and they began to buy extravagantly. I found the good man had thoroughly studied my Almanacks, and digested all I had dropt on those topicks during the course of twenty-five years. The frequent mention he made of me must have tired any one else; but my vanity was wonderfully delighted with it, tho' I was conscious, that not a tenth part of the wisdom was my own, which he ascribed to me; but rather the gleanings that I had made of the sense of all ages and nations. However, I resolved to be the better for the echo of it; and though I had at first determined to buy stuff for a new coat, I went away, resolved to wear my old one a little longer. Reader, if thou wilt do the same, thy profit will be as great as mine. I am ever thine to serve thee.

–RICHARD SAUNDERS

Advice To Young Tradesmen

by

DR. FRANKLIN

REMEMBER that time is money. He that can earn ten shillings a day by his labours and goes abroad, or sits idle one half of that day, though he spends but sixpense during his diversion or idleness, ought not to reckon that the only expense; he has really spent, or rather thrown away, five shillings besides.

Remember that credit is money. If a man lets his money lie in my hands after it is due, he gives me the interest, or so much as I can make of it during that time. This amounts to a considerable sum when a man has good and large credit, and makes good use of it.

REMEMBER that money is of a prolifick, generating nature. Many can beget money, and its offspring can beget more, and so on. Five shillings turned is six; turned again, it is seven and three pence; and so till it becomes an hundred pounds. The more there is of it, the more it produces, every turning; so that the profits rise quicker and quicker. He that kills a breeding sow, destroys all her offspring to the thousandth generation. He that murders a crown, destroys all that it might have produced, even scores of pounds.

REMEMBER that six pounds a year is but a groat a day. For this little sum, which may be daily wasted either in time or expense, unperceived, a man of credit may, on his own security, have the constant possession and use of an hundred pounds. So much in stock briskly turned by an industrious man, produces a great advantage.

REMEMBER this saying, "The good paymaster is lord of another man's purse." He that is known to pay punctually and exactly at the time he promises, may at any time, and on any occasion, raise all the money his friends can spare.

"He that kills a breeding sow, destroys all her offspring to the thousandth generation."

The way to wealth depends chiefly on INDUSTRY *and* FRUGALITY.

This is sometimes of great use. After industry and frugality, nothing contributes more to the raising of a young man in the world, than punctuality and justice in all his dealings: therefore, never keep borrowed money an hour beyond the time you promised, lest a disappointment shut your friend's purse forever.

The most trifling actions that effect a man's credit are to be regarded. The sound of your hammer at five in the morning, or nine at night, heard by a creditor, makes him easy six months longer: but if he sees you at a billiard table, or hears your voice at tavern, when you should be at work, he sends for his money the next day; demands it before he can receive it in a lump.

It shews, besides, that you are mindful of what you owe; it makes you appear a careful as well as honest man, and that still increases your credit.

Beware of thinking all your own that you possess, and of living accordingly. It is a mistake that many people, who have credit, fall into. To prevent this, keep an exact account, for some time, both of your expenses and your income. If you take the pains at first to mention particulars, it will have this good effect: you will discover how wonderfully small, trifling expenses mount up to large sums, and will discern what might have been, and may for the future be saved without occasioning any great inconvenience.

In short, the way to wealth, if you desire it, is as plain as the way to market. It depends chiefly on two words, *industry* and *frugality;* that is, waste neither *time* nor *money,* but make the best use of both. Without industry and frugality nothing will do, and with them every thing. He that gets all he can honestly, and saves all he gets, (necessary expenses excepted) will certainly become *rich,* if that Being who governs the world, to whom all should look for a blessing on their honest endeavours, doth not, in his wise providence, otherwise determine.

—An Old Tradesman

ON THE DEATH OF

DOCTOR BENJAMIN FRANKLIN

By PHILIP FRENEAU

Thus some tall tree, that long hath stood
The glory of its native wood,
By storms destroyed, or length of years,
Demands the tribute of our tears.

The pile, that took long time to raise,
To dust returns by slow decays;
But, when its destined years are o'er,
We must regret the loss the more.

So long accustomed to your aid,
The world laments your exit made;
So long befriended by your art,
Philosopher, 'tis hard to part!—

When monarchs tumble to the ground,
Successors easily are found:
But, matchless Franklin! what a few
Can hope to rival such as you,
Who seized from kings their sceptred pride,
And turned the lightning's darts aside!

*"He snatched lightning from heaven, and the scep-
ter from tyrants." This inscription in Latin appears
on a medal presented to Benjamin Franklin when he
was Ambassador to France, for the United States of
America.*

EXCERPT FROM

Epistle From Dr. Franklin (Deceased)

to his Poetical Eulogists

by PHILIP FRENEAU

"Dear Poets, why so full of pain,
Why so much grief for Doctor Ben?
Love for your tribe I never had,
Nor wrote three stanzas, good or bad.

At funerals, sometimes, grief appears,
Where legacies have purchas'd tears:
'Tis nonsense to be sad for nought,
From me you never gain'd a groat."

To better trades I turn'd my views,
And never meddled with the muse;
Great things I did for rising States,
And kept the lightning from some pates.

This grand discovery, you adore it,
But ne'er will be the better for it.
You still are subject to those fires,
For poet's houses have no spires."

*   *   *   *   *

Experience keeps a dear school, but fools will
learn in no other, and scarcely in that; for it is
true, we may give advice, but we cannot give conduct. Remember this; they that will not be coun-
seled cannot be helped. If you do not hear reason
she will rap you over your knuckles.

—FRANKLIN

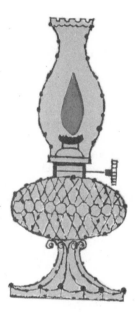

HISTORIC

The heritage of the past is the seed that brings forth the harvest of the future.
—ARCHIVES BUILDING, WASHINGTON

O grave! where is thy victory?
O death! where is thy sting?
    POPE. *The Dying Christian to his Soul.*

    Within her heart was his image,
Clothed in the beauty of love and youth,
    as last she beheld him,
Only more beautiful made by his death-
    like silence and absence.
Into her thoughts of him, time entered
    not, for it was not.
Over him years had no power; he was
    not changed, but transfigured.
    LONGFELLOW. *Evangeline.*

JOHN WINTHROP: LIBERTY HAS A DOUBLE MEANING

By JOHN WINTHROP

Born in Groton, England, Jan. 12, 1587, he was chosen by the company in London to be governor of the Massachusetts Bay Colony. He arrived in Salem, Massachusetts, June 12, 1630, and soon after settled in Boston. He served several terms as governor and his Journal of New England and other writings were published between 1630 and 1650. His son, also named John Winthrop, was also one of the prominent colonial governors.

CONCERNING liberty, I observe a great mistake in the country about that. There is a two-fold liberty, natural (I mean as our nature is now corrupt) and civil or federal. The first is common to man with beasts and other creatures. By this, man, as he stands in relation to man simply, hath liberty to do what he lists; it is a liberty to evil as well as to good. This liberty is incompatible and inconsistent with authority, and cannot endure the least restraint of the most just authority. The exercise and maintaining of this liberty makes men grow more evil, and in time to be worse than brute beasts. This is that great enemy of truth and peace, that wild beast, which all the ordinances of God are bent against, to restrain and subdue it.

The other kind of liberty I call civil or federal; it may also be termed moral, in reference to the covenant between God and man, in the moral law, and the politic covenants and constitutions, amongst men themselves. This is the proper end and object of authority, and cannot subsist without it; and it is a liberty to that only which is good, just, and honest. This liberty you are to stand for, with the hazard not only of your goods, but of your lives, if need be. Whatsoever crosseth this, is not authority, but a distemper thereof.

A day, an hour of virtuous liberty, is worth a whole eternity of bondage.

—ADDISON'S CATO

Liberty And Union Now And Forever
Daniel Webster

I profess, sir, in my career hitherto, to have kept steadily in view the prosperity and honor of the whole country, and the preservation of our federal union. It is to that union we owe our safety at home, and our consideration and dignity abroad. It is to that union that we are chiefly indebted for whatever makes us most proud of our country. That union we reached only by the discipline of our virtues in the severe school of adversity. It had its origin in the necessities of disordered finance, prostrate commerce, and ruined credit. Under its benign influences these great interests immediately awoke, as from the dead, and sprang forth with newness of life. Every year of its duration has teemed with fresh proofs of its utility and its blessings; and although our territory has stretched out wider and wider, and our population spread farther and farther, they have not outrun its protection or its benefits. It has been to us all a copious fountain of national, social, and personal happiness.

I have not allowed myself, sir, to look beyond the union, to see what might lie hidden in the dark recess behind. I have not coolly weighed the chances of preserving liberty, when the bonds that unite us together shall be broken asunder. I have not accustomed myself to hang over the precipice of disunion, to see whether, with my short sight, I can fathom the depth of the abyss below; nor could I regard him

God grants liberty only to those who love it, and are always ready to guard and defend it.
                                        —DANIEL WEBSTER

as a safe counsellor in the affairs of this government, whose thoughts should be mainly bent on considering, not how the union should be preserved, but how tolerable might be the condition of the people, when it shall be broken up and destroyed.

While the union lasts, we have high, exciting, gratifying prospects spread out before us, for us and our children. Beyond that, I seek not to penetrate the veil. God grant that in my day, at least, that curtain may not rise. God grant that on my vision never may be opened what lies behind. When my eyes shall be turned to behold for the last time the sun in heaven, may I not see him shining on the broken and dishonored fragments of a once glorious union; on states dissevered, discordant, belligerant; on a land rent with civil feuds, or drenched, it may be, in fraternal blood! Let their last feeble and lingering glance, rather, behold the gorgeous ensign of the republic, now known and honored throughout the earth, still full high advanced, its arms and trophies streaming in their original lustre; not a stripe erased or polluted, not a single star obscured,—bearing for its motto, no such miserable interrogatory as, What is all this worth? nor those other words of delusion and folly: Liberty first, and union afterwards; but everywhere, spread all over in charters of living light, blazing on all its ample folds, as they float over the sea and over the land, and in every wind under the whole heavens, that other sentiment, dear to every true American heart,—Liberty *and* union, now and forever, one and inseparable!

> *Is life so dear, or peace so sweet,*
> *as to be purchased at the price of chains*
> *and slavery? For bid it, Almighty God!*
> *I know not what course others may take,*
> *but as for me, give me liberty, or*
> *give me death.*
> —*Speech in the Virginia Convention* 1775, **PATRICK HENRY**

WHAT IS THE CONSTITUTION?

THOMAS PAINE

A CONSTITUTION is not a thing in name only, but in fact. It has not an ideal but a real existence, and wherever it cannot be produced in a visible form, there is none. A constitution is a thing antecedent to a government, and a government is only the creature of a constitution. The constitution of a country is not the act of its government, but of a people constituting a government. It is the body of elements to which you refer, and quote article by article, and contains the principles on which the government shall be established—the form in which it shall be organized—the powers it shall have—the mode of elections—the duration of Congress—and, in fine, everything that relates to the complete organization of a civil government, and the principles on which it shall act, and by which it shall be bound. A constitution is to a government, therefore, what the laws made by that government are to a court of judicature. The court of judicature does not make laws, neither can it alter them; it only acts in conformity to the laws made; and the government is in like manner governed by the constitution.

Stand fast therefore in the liberty
wherewith Christ hath made us free,
and be not entangled again with
the yoke of bondage.

Symbolism of the Colors of Old Glory

Red signifies divine love; it is the language of valor and the emblem of war.

White is the symbol of trust, of purity and the emblem of peace.

Blue is the symbol of loyalty, sincerity and justice.

GEORGE WASHINGTON'S PRAYER FOR THE UNITED STATES

Almighty God: We make our earnest prayer that Thou wilt keep the United States in Thy holy protection: that Thou wilt incline the hearts of the citizens to cultivate a spirit of subordination and obedience to government: and entertain a brotherly affection and love for one another and for their fellow citizens of the United States at large.

And finally that Thou wilt most graciously be pleased to dispose us all to do justice, to love mercy, and to demean ourselves with that charity, humility, and pacific temper of mind which were the characteristics of the Divine Author of our blessed religion, and without a humble imitation of whose example in these things we can never hope to be a happy nation.

Grant our supplication, we beseech Thee, through Jesus Christ our Lord.

AMEN

Ask, and it shall be given you; seek, and ye shall find; knock, and it shall be opened unto you.

MATTHEW VII, 7

George Washington
In the Twilight Years

Though in reviewing the incidents of my administration, I am unconscious of intentional error, I am nevertheless too sensible of my defects not to think that I may have committed many errors. Whatever they may be, I fervently beseech the Almighty to avert or mitigate the evils to which they may tend. I shall also carry with me the hope that my country will never cease to view them with indulgence and that after forty-five years of my life dedicated to its service with an upright zeal, the faults of incompetent abilities will be consigned to oblivion as myself must soon be to the mansion of rest.

The Legacy of George Washington written in 1783

1. All the states must be under one federal government.
2. All debts incurred by the war must be paid to the utmost farthing.
3. The militia system must be organized under uniform principles.
4. All people must be willing to sacrifice, if necessary, their local interests to the common weal, and regard themselves fellow-citizens of a common country.

THOMAS JEFFERSON'S
RULES OF LIVING

NEVER put off till tomorrow what you can do today.
Never trouble another for what you can do yourself.
Never spend your money before you have it.
Never buy what you do not want because it is cheap.
Pride costs us more than hunger, thirst, and cold.
We seldom repent having eaten too little.
Nothing is troublesome that we do willingly.
How much pain the evils have cost us that have never
   happened!
Take things always by the smooth handle.
When angry, count ten before you speak: if very angry, a
   hundred.

Know then thyself, presume not God to scan;
The proper study of mankind is man.

—ALEXANDER POPE

DESCRIPTION OF
Thomas Jefferson: Patriarch

A Visit to Monticello in 1824

by DANIEL WEBSTER

From *The Writings and Speeches of Daniel Webster,* edited by Fletcher Webster (Volume 17), Boston, 1903. Taken from JEFFERSON READER, Published by E. P. Dutton & Co., New York.

MR. JEFFERSON is now between eighty-one and eighty-two, above six feet high, of an ample long frame, rather thin and spare. His head, which is not peculiar in its shape, is set rather forward on his shoulders; and his neck being long, there is, when he is walking or conversing, an habitual protrusion of it. It is still well covered with hair, which having once been red, and now turning gray, is of an indistinct sandy color.

His eyes are small, very light, and now neither brilliant nor striking. His chin is rather long, but not pointed. His nose small, regular in its outline, and the nostrils a little elevated. His mouth is well formed and still filled with teeth; it is strongly compressed, bearing an expression of contentment and bears the marks of age and cutaneous affection. His limbs are uncommonly long; his hands and feet very large, and his wrists of an extraordinary size. His walk is not precise and military, but easy and swinging. He stoops a little, not so much from age as from a natural formation. When sitting, he appears short, partly from a rather lounging habit of sitting, and partly from the disproportionate length of his limbs.

His dress, when in the house, is a gray surtout coat, kerseymere stuff waistcoat, with an under one faced with some material of a dingy red. His pantaloons are very long and loose, and of the same color as his coat. His stockings are woollen either white or gray; and his shoes of the kind that bear his name. His whole dress is very much neglected, but not slovenly. He wears a common round hat. His dress, when on horseback, is a gray straight-bodied coat and a spencer of the same material, both fastened with large pearl buttons. When we first saw him, he was riding; and, in addition to the above articles of apparel, wore round his throat a knit white woollen tippet, in the place of a cravat, and black velvet gaiters under his pantaloons. His general appearance indicates an extraordinary degree of health, vivacity, and spirit. His sight is still good, for he needs glasses only in the evening. His hearing is generally good, but a number of voices in animated conversation confuses it.

Mr. Jefferson rises in the morning as soon as he can see the hands of his clock, which is directly opposite his bed, and examines his thermometer immediately, as he keeps a regular meteorological diary. He employs himself chiefly in writing till breakfast, which is at nine. From that time, till dinner, he is in his library, excepting that in fair weather he rides on horseback from seven to fourteen miles. Dines at four, returns to the drawing-room at six, when coffee is brought in, and passes the evening till nine in conversation. His habit of retiring at that hour is so strong, that it has become essential to his health and comfort. His diet is simple, but he seems restrained only by his taste. His breakfast is tea and coffee, bread always fresh from the oven, of which he does not seem afraid, with sometimes a slight accompaniment of cold meat. He enjoys his dinner well, taking with his meat a large portion of vegetables. He has a strong preference for the wines of the continent, of which he has many sorts of excellent quality, having been more than commonly successful in his mode of importing and preserving them. Among others, we found the following, which are very rare in this country, and apparently not at all injured by transportation: L'Ednau, Muscat, Samian, and Blanchette de Limoux. Dinner is served in half Virginian, half French style, in good taste and abundance. No wine is put on the table till the cloth is removed.

In conversation, Mr. Jefferson is easy and natural, and apparently not ambitious; it is not loud, as challenging general attention, but usually addressed to the person next him. The topics, when not selected to suit the character and feelings of his auditor, are those subjects with which his mind seems particularly occupied; and these, at present, may be said to be science and letters, and especially the University of Virginia, which is coming into existence almost entirely from his exertions, and will rise, it is to be hoped, to usefulness and credit under his continued care. When we were with him, his favorite subjects were Greek and Anglo-Saxon, historical recollections of the times and events of the Revolution, and of his residence in France from 1783-4 to 1789.

THOMAS JEFFERSON
ETERNAL FOE OF TYRANNY

I AM not an advocate for frequent changes in laws and constitutions. But laws and institutions must go hand in hand with the progress of the human mind as that becomes more developed, more enlightened, as new discoveries are made, new truths discovered and manners and opinions change, with the change of circumstance, institutions must advance also to keep pace with the times. We might as well require a man to wear still the coat which fitted him when a boy, as civilized society to remain ever under the regimen of their barbarous ancestors.

I have sworn upon the altar of God eternal hostility against every form of tyranny over the mind of man.

Freedom of religion; freedom of the press; freedom of person under the protection of the habeas corpus.

—*First inaugural address,* THOMAS JEFFERSON

Captain Cook Resolute Voyager

Captain James Cook, the celebrated English navigator, was killed on Hawaii in 1779. Since his explorations largely opened the Sandwich Islands (Hawaii) to the Western World, a description of the man by one of his associates seems both timely and interesting in this year of Hawaiian statehood. Take from the original printing of A Voyage to the Pacific Ocean *by James Cook, F.R.S. and Captain James King, LL.P. and F.R.S. 1793.*

His frame and constitution were robust, and such as enabled him to undergo the severest hardships. When necessity required it, he could feed, with satisfaction, upon the coarsest and most ungrateful food; and he submitted to every kind of self-denial with the greatest composure and indifference. Nor were the qualities of his mind less vigorous than those of his body. His understanding was strong and perspicuous: his judgment, especially in those matters in which he was more particularly engaged, quick and sure. His designs and operations, were the natural result of a great original genius. His valour was cool, deliberate, and determined; accompanied with a most astonishing presence of mind on the approach of danger. His manners were plain, easy, and unaffected. His temper, it must be admitted, was too much subject to hastiness and passion; but this should be forgotten, when it is considered, that this disposition was the most benevolent and humane.

These are a few traits or outlines of the character of Captain Cook; but its distinguishing feature was, the most unremitting perseverance to accomplish his design, in opposition to dangers, difficulties and hardships. During all his long and tedious voyages, his eagerness and activity were never in the least abated. No alluring incitement could detain him for a moment; even those intervals of recreation, which unavoidably occurred in the course of our services, and were joyfully embraced by many of his officers, were submitted to by him with impatience, if they could not be made subservient to the more effectual prosecution of his designs.

It would be unnecessary to recapitulate the instances in which these qualities were displayed. The result of his services, however, we shall just touch upon, under two principal heads, viz. geography and navigation, placing each in a separate and distinct point of view.

No science, it is presumed, has even received greater additions from the labours of one man, than geography has done from those of Captain Cook. In his first voyage, he discovered the Society Islands; ascertained the insularity of New Zealand; and discovered the straits which separate the two islands, and are called after his name. He explored the eastern coast of New Holland, till then unknown; an extent of twenty-seven degrees of latitude, and upwards of two thousand miles.

He gave, in his second expedition, a resolution to the great problem of a southern continent; having so completely traversed that hemisphere, as not to leave a possibility of its existence, unless it is so near the pole, as to be beyond the reach of navigation. New Caledonia, the largest island in the Southern Pacific, except New Zealand, was discovered in this voyage. Also the island of Georgia; and an unknown coast, which the Captain named Sandwich land; and having twice visited the tropical seas, he settled the situations of the old, and made several new discoveries.

His third and last voyage, however, is distinguished above the rest, by the extent and importance of its discoveries. Not to mention the several smaller islands in the Southern Pacific, he discovered the group, called the Sandwich islands; which, on account of their situation and productions, may perhaps become an object of more consequence than any other discovery in the South Sea. He explored what had before remained unknown of the western coast of America, an extent of three thousand seven hundred miles; ascertained the proximity of the two continents of Asia and America; sailed through the straits between them, and surveyed the coasts on each side, so far as to be satisfied of the impracticability of a passage in that hemisphere, from the Atlantic into the Pacific Ocean, by an eastern or western course. He has, in short, compleated the hydrography of the habitable globe, if we except the Japanese Archipelago, and the sea of Amur, which are still imperfectly known by Europeans.

LINCOLN, MAN OF STEEL AND VELVET

By CARL SANDBURG

We are in the centennial anniversary of the Lincoln era. The distinguished biographer and poet, Carl Sandburg, is best qualified to point out why this remarkable man is respected as one of the giants of the ages.

NOT OFTEN IN THE STORY of mankind does a man arrive on earth who is both steel and velvet, who is as hard as rock and soft as drifting fog, who holds in his heart and mind the paradox of terrible storm and peace unspeakable and perfect.

Here and there across centuries come reports of men alleged to have these contrasts. And the incomparable Abraham Lincoln, born 150 years ago this day, is an approach if not a perfect realization of this character.

In the time of the April lilacs in the year 1865, on his death, the casket with his body was carried north and west a thousand miles; and the American people wept as never before; bells sobbed; cities wore crape; people stood in tears and with hats off as the railroad burial car paused in the leading cities of seven States, ending its journey at Springfield, Illinois, the home town.

DURING THE FOUR YEARS he was President, he at times, especially in the first three months, took to himself the powers of a dictator; he commanded the most powerful armies till then assembled in modern warfare; he enforced conscription of soldiers for the first time in American history; under imperative necessity he abolished the right of habeas corpus; he directed politically and spiritually the wild, massive, turbulent forces let loose in civil war. He argued and pleaded for compensated emancipation of the slaves.

The slaves were property; they were on the tax books along with horses and cattle, the valuation of each slave written next to his name on the tax assessor's books. Failing to get action on compensated emancipation, as a Chief Executive having war powers he issued the paper by which he declared the slaves to be free under "military necessity." In the end nearly four billion dollars' worth of property was taken away from those who were legal owners of it—property confiscated, wiped out as by fire and turned to ashes, at his instigation and executive direction. Chattel property recognized and lawful for 250 years was expropriated, seized without payment.

In the month the war began, he told his secretary, John Hay, "My policy is to have no policy." Three years later in a letter to a Kentucky friend made public, he confessed plainly, "I have been controlled by events."

His WORDS AT GETTYSBURG were sacred, yet strange with a color of the familiar: "We can not consecrate —we can not hallow—this ground. The brave men, living and dead, who struggled here, have consecrated it, far above our poor power to add or detract."

He could have said "The brave Union men." Did he have a purpose in omitting the word "Union"? Was he keeping himself and his utterance clear of the passion that would not be good to look back on when the time came for peace and reconciliation? Did he mean to leave an implication that there were brave Union men and brave Confederate men, living and dead, who had struggled there? We do not know, of a certainty.

Was he thinking of the Kentucky father whose two sons died in battle, one in Union blue, the other in Confederate gray, the father inscribing on the stone over their double grave, "God knows which was right"? We do not know.

His changing policies from time to time always aimed at saving the Union. In the end his armies won and his Nation became a world power.

In August of 1864 he wrote a memorandum that, in view of the national situation, he expected to lose the next November election; that month of August was so dark. Sudden military victory brought the tide his way; the vote was

2,200,000 for him and 1,800,000 against him. Among his bitter opponents were such figures as Samuel F. B. Morse, inventor of the telegraph, and Cyrus H. McCormick, inventor of the farm reaper. In all its essential propositions the Southern Confederacy had the moral support of powerful, respectable elements throughout the North, probably more than a million voters believing in the justice of the Southern cause.

While the war winds howled, he insisted that the Mississippi was one river meant to belong to one country, that railroad connection from coast to coast must be pushed through and the Union Pacific Railroad made a reality.

While the luck of war wavered and broke and came again, as generals failed and campaigns were lost, he held enough forces of the North together to raise new armies and supply them, until generals were found who made war as victorious war has always been made, with terror, frightfulness, destruction, and on both sides, North and South, valor and sacrifice past words of man to tell.

In the mixed shame and blame of the immense wrongs of two crashing civilizations, often with nothing to say, he said nothing, slept not at all, and on occasions he was seen to weep in a way that made weeping appropriate, decent, majestic.

AS HE RODE ALONE on horseback near Soldiers' Home on the edge of Washington one night, his hat was shot off; a son he loved died as he watched at the bed; his wife was accused of betraying information to the enemy, until denials from him were necessary.

An Indiana man at the White House heard him say, "Voorhees, don't it seem strange to you that I, who could never so much as cut off the head of a chicken, should be elected, or selected, into the midst of all this blood?"

He tried to guide Gen. Nathaniel Prentiss Banks, three times Governor of Massachusetts, in the governing of some 17 of the 48 parishes of Louisiana controlled by the Union armies, an area holding a fourth of the slaves of Louisiana. He would like to see the State recognize the Emancipation

Proclamation: "And while she is at it, I think it would not be objectionable for her to adopt some practical system by which the two races could gradually live themselves out of their old relation to each other, and both come out better prepared for the new. Education for young blacks should be included in the plan."

To Gov. Michael Hahn, elected in 1864 by a majority of the 11,000 white male voters who had taken the oath of allegiance to the Union, Lincoln wrote: "Now you are about to have a Convention which, among other things, will probably define the elective franchise. I barely suggest . . . whether some of the colored people may not be let in—as, for instance, the very intelligent, and especially those who have fought gallantly in our ranks."

AMONG THE MILLION WORDS in the Lincoln utterance record, he interprets himself with a more keen precision than someone else offering to explain him. His simple opening of the House Divided speech in 1858 serves for today: "If we could first know *where* we are, and *whither* we are tending, we could then better judge *what* to do, and *how* to do it."

To his Kentucky friend, Joshua F. Speed, he wrote in 1855: "Our progress in degeneracy appears to me to be pretty rapid. As a nation, we began by declaring that '*all men are created equal*.' We now practically read it 'all men are created equal, *except negroes*.' When the Know-Nothings get control, it will read 'all men are created equal, except negroes, *and foreigners, and catholics*.' When it comes to this I should prefer emigrating to some country where they make no pretense of loving liberty."

Infinitely tender was his word from a White House balcony to a crowd on the White House lawn, "I have not will-

One of the people! born to be
Their curious epitome;
To share yet rise above
Their shifting hate and love.
Abraham Lincoln, RICHARD HENRY STODDARD

ingly planted a thorn in any man's bosom," or to a military governor, "I shall do nothing through malice; what I deal with is too vast for malice."

He wrote for Congress to read on December 1, 1862: "In times like the present, men should utter nothing for which they would not willingly be responsible through time and in eternity." Like an ancient psalmist he warned Congress: "Fellow-citizens, *we* cannot escape history. We . . . will be remembered in spite of ourselves. No personal significance, or insignificance, can spare one or another of us. The fiery trial through which we pass, will light us down, in honor or dishonor, to the latest generation."

Wanting Congress to break and forget past traditions, his words came keen and flashing: "The dogmas of the quiet past, are inadequate to the stormy present. . . . We must think anew, and act anew. We must disenthrall ourselves." They are the sort of words that actuated the mind and will of the men who created and navigated that marvel of the sea, the *Nautilus*, on her voyage from Pearl Harbor and under the North Pole icecap.

The people of many other countries take Lincoln now for their own. He belongs to them. He stands for decency, honest dealing, plain talk, and funny stories. "Look where he came from—don't he know all us strugglers and wasn't he a kind of tough struggler all his life right up to the finish?" Something like that you can hear in any near-by neighborhood and across the seas.

Millions there are who take him as a personal treasure. He had something they would like to see spread everywhere over the world.

Democracy? We can't say exactly what it is, but he had it. In his blood and bones he carried it. In the breath of his speeches and writings it is there.

Popular government? Republican institutions? Government where the people have the say-so, one way or another telling their elected leaders what they want? He had the

Our children shall behold his fame,
The kindly, earnest, brave, foreseeing man—
Commemoration Ode, JAMES RUSSELL LOWELL

idea. It is there in the lights and shadows of his personality, a mystery that can be lived but never fully spoken in words.

Our good friend, the poet and playwright Mark Van Doren, tells us, "To me, Lincoln seems, in some ways, the most interesting man who ever lived. He was gentle, but this gentleness was combined with a terrific toughness, an iron strength."

How DID LINCOLN SAY he would like to be remembered? Something of it is in this present occasion, the atmosphere of this room. His beloved friend, Representative Owen Lovejoy, of Illinois, had died in May of 1864, and friends wrote to Lincoln and he replied that the pressure of duties kept him from joining them in efforts for a marble monument to Lovejoy, the last sentence of Lincoln's letter saying:

"Let him have the marble monument, along with the well-assured and more enduring one in the hearts of those who love liberty, unselfishly, for all men."

Today we may say, perhaps, that the well-assured and most enduring memorial to Lincoln is invisibly there, today, tomorrow, and for a long time yet to come. It is there in the hearts of lovers of liberty, men and women—this country has always had them in crisis—men and women who understand that wherever there is freedom there have been those who fought, toiled, and sacrificed for it.

Here the free spirit of mankind at length
Throws its last fetters off; and who shall place
A limit to the giant's unchained strength,
Or curb his swiftness in the forward race?

William Cullen Bryant

HYMN

AFTER THE EMANCIPATION
PROCLAMATION

Oliver Wendell Holmes

Giver of all that crowns our days,
With Grateful hearts we sing Thy praise!
Through deep and desert led by Thee
Our Canaan's promised land we see.

Ruler of Nations, judge our cause!
If we have kept Thy Holy laws,
The sons of Belial curse in vain
The day that rends the captives' chain.

Thou God of vengeance! Israel's Lord!
Break in their grasp the shield and sword,
And make Thy righteous judgments known
Till all Thy foes are overthrown!

Then, Father, lay Thy healing hand
In mercy on our stricken land;
Lead all its wanderers to the fold,
And be their Shepherd as of old!

So shall one Nation's song ascend
to Thee, our Ruler, Father, Friend;
While Heaven's wide arch resounds again
With Peace on earth, good will to men!

*There is nothing wrong with America that the faith,
love of freedom, intelligence and energy of her
citizens cannot cure.* — Dwight D. Eisenhower

Headquarters Armies of the United States

City Point, April 7, 11 A.M. 1865

LIEUT. GEN. GRANT

Gen. Sheridan says "If the thing is pressed I think that Lee will surrender." Let the thing be pressed.

A. LINCOLN

Dispatch sent by Mr. Lincoln to me Apl. 7th, 1865.

U. S. GRANT

THE CHARACTER OF ROBERT E. LEE

From *Personal Reminiscences of General
Robert E. Lee* by J. WILLIAM JONES, D.D.

HE POSSESSED every virtue of the great commanders,
without their vices. He was a foe without hate; a friend
without treachery; a private citizen without wrong; a neigh-
bor without reproach; a Christian without hypocrisy, and
a man without guilt. He was a Caesar without his ambition;
a Frederick without his tyranny; a Napoleon without his
selfishness; and a Washington without his reward. He was
obedient to authority as a servant, and loyal in authority as
a true king. He was gentle as a woman in life; modest and
pure as a virgin in thought; watchful as a Roman vestal in
duty; submissive to law as Socrates, and grand in battle as
Achilles.

"There were many peculiarities in the habits and character of Lee which are but little known, and may be studied
with profit. He studiously avoided giving opinions upon
subjects which it had not been his calling or training to
investigate; and sometimes I thought he carried this great
virtue too far. Neither the President, nor Congress, nor
friends, could get his views upon any public question not
strictly military, and no man had as much quiet, unobtru-
sive contempt for what he called 'military statesmen and
political generals.' Meeting him once on the streets of Richmond, I said to him, 'General, I wish you would give us your
opinion as to the propriety of changing the seat of government and going farther south.'

" 'That is a political question, Mr. Hill, and you politicians must determine it; I shall endeavor to take care of the
army, and you must make the laws and control the government.'

*Misfortunes display the skill of a general, prosper-
ous circumstances conceal his weakness.*—HORACE

IMMORTAL WORDS
IN ANY AGE —

The brief address, embodying Lincoln's hopes for peace and reconstruction, was called by the London Times "the most sublime State paper of the century" and was described by Charles Francis Adams, the younger, as "for all time the historical keynote of this war." Of it, Lincoln, himself wrote: "I expect (it) to wear as well as . . . perhaps better than anything I have produced; but I believe it is not immediately popular. Men are not flattered by being shown that there has been a difference of purpose between the Almighty and them. To deny it, however, in this case is to deny that there is a God governing the world. . . ."

This is a reference to the Second Inaugural Address (March 4, 1865) which closed with these three paragraphs:

F ONDLY do we hope—fervently do we pray—that this mighty scourge of war may speedily pass away.

Yet if God wills that it continue until all the wealth piled by the bondsman's two hundred and fifty years of unrequited toil shall be sunk, and until every drop of blood drawn with the lash shall be paid by another drawn with the sword, as was said three thousand years ago, so still it must be said, "the judgments of the Lord are true and righteous altogether."

With malice toward none; with charity for all; with firmness in the right, as God gives us to see the right, let us strive on to finish the work we are in; to bind up the nation's wounds; to care for him who shall have borne the battle, and for his widow and his orphan—to do all which may achieve and cherish a just and a lasting peace among ourselves and with all nations.

It is by the goodness of God that in our country we have these three unspeakably precious things: freedom of speech, freedom of conscience and the prudence never to practice either of them.

—MARK TWAIN

Abraham Lincoln Quotes from Hamlet
In Giving Advice to An Officer
Guilty of Misconduct

ADVICE TO an erring officer, Captain James Madison Cutts, Jr., brother-in-law of Stephen A. Douglas, who at a court martial was found guilty of "conduct unbecoming an officer and a gentleman."

October 26, 1863

Although what I am now to say is to be in a form a reprimand, it is not intended to add a pang to what you have already suffered upon the whole subject to which it relates.

You have too much of life yet before you, and have shown too much of promise as an officer, for your future to be lightly surrendered.

You were convicted of two offenses. One of them not of great enormity, and yet greatly to be avoided, I feel sure you are in no danger of repeating. The other you are not so well assured against. The advice of a father to his son, "Beware of entrance to a quarrel, but being in, bear't that the opposed may beware of thee," is good, and yet not the best. Quarrel not at all. No man resolved to make the most of himself can spare time for personal contention. Still less can he afford to take all the consequences, including the vitiating of his temper, and the loss of self control.

*Giving advice is a very peculiar affair; and when one has looked round the world for a time and seen how the most cleverly designed enterprises fail, and how the most absurd often turn out well, one becomes chary of giving any one advice. There is, at bottom, a certain restraint in him who asks for counsel, and an overweening feeling of superiority in him who gives it. One should only advise about matters in which one is prepared to cooperate.—*GOETHE.

INSCRIBED FOR THE AGES
BY THE AGES

THE following quotation is carved in the marble wall beneath the memorial medallion of Andrew W. Mellon, erected by order of the Board of Trustees, in the lobby of the north entrance of the National Gallery of Art:

"For the whole earth is the
sepulchre of famous men and
their story is not graven
only on stone over their
native earth but lives on
far away without visible
symbol woven into the stuff
of other men's lives."

The medallion showing the profile of Andrew W. Mellon is the work of the American sculptor, Walker Hancock. The inscription above, translated from the Greek by Alfred W. Zimmern, is from the Oration of Pericles over the dead in the Peloponnesian War and was delivered at Athens in 430 B. C. After the Athenians had suffered several reverses, Pericles made this great appeal to the pride of his countrymen and praised the warriors who had fallen in their country's service. Pericles' Oration is given in full in Thucydides, *The History of the Peloponnesian War*, Book II, 35 et seq.

Great truths are portions of the soul of man;
Great souls are portions of eternity.
—Sonnet VI, JAMES RUSSELL LOWELL

POET OF THE CONFEDERACY

During the years of the nineteen sixties there will be many observances of the centennial anniversary of occurrences of the war between the States. Other than the military aspects there were cultural and literary developments of that period worthy of notice. The gifted Sidney Lanier left a heritage of beautiful and unusual poetry —

SIDNEY LANIER was born in Macon, Georgia, February 3, 1842. His earliest known ancestor was attached to the court of Queen Elizabeth, very likely as a musical composer. Others in his family had distinguished music backgrounds. The American branch of the family originated in 1716 with the immigration of Thomas Lanier, who settled with other colonists on a grant of land ten miles square, which includes the present city of Richmond, Virginia. Sidney, as a child, learned to play, almost without instruction, the flute, organ, piano, violin, guitar and banjo. During his college days at Oglethorpe, the violin would at times so entrance him, he would sink into a deep trance and awake alone on the floor of his room, his nerves badly shaken.

He served with the Confederate Army in the signal service because of his flute playing. The tyranny and Christlessness of war oppressed him. His writing began immediately after his release from Point Lookout in 1865. He expressed himself more with the style of music than with literature. His career was shortened by consumption, to which he succumbed September 7, 1881. Yet, he was one of the true geniuses of the nineteenth century. His poems and writings have the spirit of today and tomorrow — not of yesterday.

Souls and Rain-Drops

by SIDNEY LANIER

Light rain-drops fall and wrinkle the sea,
Then vanish, and die utterly.
One would not know that rain-drops fell
If the round sea-wrinkles did not tell.

So souls come down and wrinkle life
And vanish in the flesh-sea strife.
One might not know that souls had place
Were 't not for the wrinkles in life's face.

WEDDING HYMN

SIDNEY LANIER   MACON, GEORGIA   1865

Thou God, whose high, eternal Love
  Is the only blue sky of our life,
Clear all the Heaven that bends above
  The life-road of this man and wife.

May these two lives be but one note
  In the world's strange-sounding harmony,
Whose sacred music e'er shall float
  Through every discord up to Thee.

As when from separate stars two beams
  Unite to form one tender ray:
As when two sweet but shadowy dreams
  Explain each other in the day:

So may these two dear hearts one light
  Emit, and each interpret each.
Let an angel come and dwell to-night
  In this dear double-heart, and teach!

A SONG OF THE FUTURE

SIDNEY LANIER   BALTIMORE   1878

Sail fast, sail fast,
Ark of my hopes, Ark of my dreams;
Sweep lordly o'er the drowned Past,
Fly glittering through the sun's strange beams;
Sail fast, sail fast.
Breaths of new buds from off some drying lea
With news about the Future scent the sea:
My brain is beating like the heart of Haste;
I'll loose me a bird upon this Present waste;
Go, trembling song,
And stay not long; oh, stay not long:
Thou 'rt only a gray and sober dove,
But thine eye is faith and thy wing is love.

The New World Gives the Old World a Second Chance

Reprinted by permission from THINK MAGAZINE, *Copyright 1959, by* INTERNATIONAL BUSINESS MACHINES CORPORATION.

WESTERN man has known two prodigious revolutions in the past 1,000 years.

One revolution produced America—the revolution that broke up the medieval world, shattered the "universal" church, humanized and secularized the thought of man, introduced modern science and even modern technology, shifted the center of gravity from the Mediterranean to the Atlantic, and opened up a New World. All of this was the necessary background to the discovery of America, and better than any other single event the discovery of America marks the dividing line between the medieval and the modern world.

The second great revolution, America herself inaugurated and inspired. It is no less fundamental than that of the 15th and 16th centuries, and more far-reaching. It is the revolution of our time, the revolution that we associate with the end of colonialism, the emergence of a score of new nations claiming equality with the old, the spread of the principles of self-government across the globe, the use of science and technology to replace an economy of scarcity with an economy of abundance, the shift in the center of gravity from the western to the eastern hemisphere.

As the future of Europe was bound up, in so many ways, with the first revolution, so the future of America is bound up, inextricably, with the second. European civilization triumphed in the New World: it was the New World that provided European man with a second chance; it was the New. World that, in its own heterogeneous population, recreated European unity; it was the New World that, in Winston Churchill's great phrase, "stepped forth to the rescue and liberation of the Old." And it may well be that American civilization will triumph, in turn, in the new world of Asia and Africa and South America that is coming up so rapidly over the historical horizon.

The Functions Of A University

by THEODORE ROOSEVELT

"A great university like this has two special functions. The first is to produce a small number of scholars of the highest rank, a small number of men who, in science and literature, or in art, will do productive work of the first class. The second is to send out into the world a very large number of men who could never achieve and who ought not to try to achieve such a position in the field of scholarship, but whose energies are to be felt in every other form of activity; and who should go out from our doors with the balanced development of body, of mind, and above all, of character, which shall fit them to do work both honorable and efficient."

No man ever reached to excellence in any one art or profession without having passed through the slow and painful process of study and preparation. —HORACE

'Tis education forms the common mind; just as the twig is bent the tree's inclined.

ALEXANDER POPE: *Essay on Man*

Beauty

Beauty without virtue is like a flower without perfume.

All are but parts of one stupendous
  whole,
Whose body Nature is, and God the
  soul;
That, changed through all, and yet in
  all the same;
Great in the earth, as in the ethereal
  frame;
Warms in the sun, refreshes in the
  breeze,
Glows in the stars, and blossoms in the
  trees,
Lives through all life, extends through
  all extent,
Spreads undivided, operates unspent;
Breathes in our soul, informs our mortal
  part,
As full as perfect, in a hair as heart;
As full, as perfect, in vile Man that
  mourns,
As the rapt seraph, that adores and
  burns:
To Him no high, no low, no great, no
  small;
He fills, He bounds, connects, and equals
  all.

    Pope. *Essay on Man. Epistle i. l. 269.*

Our Friend, the Tree

From a booklet prepared by the Northeastern Forest Experiment Station of the U.S. Forest Service

LATELY man has shown concern for the future of Mother Earth. He has expressed concern that his own existence may be threatened by breathing noxious air, listening to earsplitting noise, drinking foul water and viewing graceless landscapes.

In the midst of the environmental uproar, the Tree stands by—like a faithful watchdog—dispensing life-giving benefits and lives on—like a silent lapdog—taken for granted, and yet one of man's best friends.

*   *   *

Trees help supply oxygen we need to breathe. Yearly, each acre of young trees can produce enough oxygen to keep eighteen people alive...

Trees help keep our air supply fresh by using up carbon dioxide that we exhale and that factories and engines emit...

Trees use their hairy leaf surfaces to trap and filter out ash, dust and pollen particles carried in the air...

Trees dilute gaseous pollutants in the air as they release oxygen...

Trees can be used to indicate air pollution levels of sulfur dioxide, just as canaries were once used to detect dangerous methane gas in coal mines...

Trees provide food for birds and wild animals...

Trees lower air temperatures by enlisting the sun's energy to evaporate water in the leaves...

Trees increase humidity in dry climates by releasing moisture as a by-product of food-making and evaporation...

Trees give us a constant supply of products—lumber for buildings and tools, cellulose for paper and fiber; as well as nuts, mulches, oils, gums, syrups and fruits...

Trees slow down forceful winds...

Trees cut noise pollution by acting as barriers to sound. Each 100-foot width of trees can absorb about 6 to 8 decibels of sound intensity. Along busy highways, which can generate as much as 72 decibels, this reduction would be welcome to residents...

Trees provide shelter for birds and wildlife and even for us when caught in a rain shower without an umbrella...

Trees shade us from direct sunlight better than any sombrero. They are welcome in parking lots on hot sunny days...

Tree leaves, when fallen, cover the ground to keep the soil from drying out...

Trees camouflage harsh scenery and unsightly city dumps, auto graveyards, and mine sites...

Trees offer a natural challenge to youthful climbers . . .

Trees make excellent perches for Robinson Crusoe-style playhouses . . .

Tree branches support ruggedly-used swings . . .

Tree leaves break the onslaught of pelting raindrops on the soil surface and give the soil a chance to soak up as much water as possible . . .

Tree leaves, by decaying, replace minerals in the soil and enrich it to support later plant growth . . .

Tree roots hold the soil and keep silt from washing into streams . . .

Tree roots help air get beneath the soil surface...

Trees salve the psyche with pleasing shapes and patterns, fragrant blossoms and seasonal splashes of color . . .

Trees break the monotony of endless sidewalks and miles of highways . . .

Trees beautify our gardens and grace our backyards . . .

Trees soften the outline of the masonry, metal and glass cityscape . . .

And Trees provide for America's economic growth and stability.

The House By The Side Of The Road

by

SAM WALTER FOSS

There are hermit souls that live withdrawn
In the place of their self-content;
There are souls like stars, that dwell apart,
In a fellowless firmament;
There are pioneer souls that blaze their paths
Where highways never ran—
But let me live by the side of the road
And be a friend to man.

Let me live in a house by the side of the road,
Where the race of men go by—
The men who are good and the men who are bad,
As good and as bad as I.
I would not sit in the scorner's seat,
Or hurl the cynic's ban—
Let me live in a house by the side of the road
And be a friend to man.

I see from my house by the side of the road,
By the side of the highway of life,
The men who press with the ardor of hope,
The men who are faint with the strife.
But I turn not away from their smiles nor their tears,
Both parts of an infinite plan—
Let me live in a house by the side of the road
And be a friend to man.

> 'Tis something to be willing to commend;
> But my best praise, is, that I am your friend.
> —To Mr. Congreve on the Old Bachelor, SOUTHERNE

I know there are brook-gladdened meadows ahead,
And mountains of wearisome height;
That the road passes on through the long afternoon
And stretches away to the night.
But still I rejoice when the travelers rejoice,
And weep with the strangers that moan,
Nor live in my house by the side of the road
Like a man who dwells alone.

Let me live in my house by the side of the road,
Where the race of men go by—
They are good, they are bad, they are weak, they are strong,
Wise, foolish—so am I;
Then why should I sit in the scorner's seat,
Or hurl the cynic's ban?
Let me live in my house by the side of the road
And be a friend to man.

Reaching the Truth Requires
Much Searching

by ALDEN WHITMAN

Margaret Bourke-White became the outstanding photojournalist among women during the 1930s and the World War II years. She established her own career among leading professionals in her field without regard to sex, wealth, or political influence. In 1936 she was a member of the original staff of Life magazine, for whose first issue she took pictures of Fort Peck Dam in Montana. On August 27, 1971 she passed away at the age of sixty-seven, after many years of patiently suffering from Hodgkin's disease. This excerpt from her obituary in the New York Times of August 28, 1971 expresses some of the dynamism manifested by this worthy forerunner of the Women's Liberation Movement.

AGGRESSIVE and relentless in pursuit of pictures, Maggie, as Miss Bourke-White was generally known, had the knack of being at the right place at the right time. For example, she interviewed and photographed Mohandas K. Gandhi a few hours before his assassination in India. And she was the only American photographer in the Soviet Union in 1941 while the battle for Moscow raged.

Many of the world's notables sat for her shutter—President Franklin D. Roosevelt, Winston Churchill (who gave her just twelve minutes), Emperor Haile Selassie, Pope Pius XI, and Stalin.

For her meeting with Stalin in the Kremlin in 1941, which was arranged by Harry Hopkins, Miss Bourke-White employed a stratagem to catch him off guard. Recalling the incident, she wrote:

"I made up my mind that I wouldn't leave without getting a picture of Stalin smiling. When I met him, his face looked as though it were carved out of stone. He wouldn't show any emotion at all. I went virtually berserk trying to make that 'great stone face' come alive.

"I got down on my hands and knees on the floor and tried out all kinds of crazy postures searching for a good camera angle. Stalin looked down at the way I was squirming and writhing and for the space of a lightning flash he smiled—and I got my picture. Probably, he had never seen a girl photographer before and my weird contortions amused him."

Miss Bourke-White often maintained that a woman shouldn't trade on the fact that she is a woman. Nonetheless, several of her male colleagues were certain that her fetching looks—she was tall, slim, dark-haired and possessed of a beautiful face—were often employed to her advantage.

"Generals rushed to tote her cameras," Mr. Eisenstadt recalled, "and even Stalin insisted on carrying her bags."

Truth is essential

"I feel that utter truth is essential," Miss Bourke-White said of her work, "and to get that truth may take a lot of searching and long hours."

In practice, this attitude resulted in pictures of starkness and simplicity, but that were withal infused with a sense of humanity. Her photographs of the American sharecroppers, presented in "You Have Seen Their Faces," captured the tragedy and desolation of the rural United States in the nineteen-thirties. The cracked and parched earth seemed one with the lined and weathered faces of the Depression's victims.

Miss Bourke-White became a photographer by necessity. Born in New York on June 14, 1904, she was the daughter of Joseph and Minnie Bourke-White. Her father was a naturalist, engineer and inventor. She attended six colleges, winding up at Cornell. Meantime, her father had died and after a marriage at nineteen had broken up, Miss Bourke-White was obliged to support herself.

She turned to taking pictures with a second-hand, twenty dollar Ica Reflex that had a crack straight through the lens. Her first painfully taken photographs of Cornell's spectacular Ithaca campus, sold well enough to encourage her to become a professional photographer. She made her first reputation in Cleveland as an architectural and industrial photographer. Arriving in the Lake Erie city by boat, she said:

"I stood on the deck to watch the city come into view. As the skyline took form in the morning mist, I felt I was coming to my promised land—columns of machinery gaining height as we drew toward the pier, derricks swinging like living creatures. Deep inside I knew these were my subjects."

BREATHES THERE THE MAN

by

SIR WALTER SCOTT

Breathes there the man with soul so dead
Who never to himself hath said,
    This is my own, my native land!
Whose heart hath ne'er within him burned,
As home his footsteps he hath turned
    From wandering on a foreign strand!
If such there breathe, go, mark him well;
For him no minstrel raptures swell;
High though his titles, proud his name,
Boundless his wealth as wish can claim,
Despite those titles, power, and pelf,
The wretch, concentred all in self,
Living, shall forfeit fair renown,
And, doubly dying, shall go down
To the vile dust from whence he sprung,
Unwept, unhonored, and unsung.

THE WAY OF THE WORLD

by

ELLA WHEELER WILCOX

Laugh and the world laughs with you;
  Weep and you weep alone
This grand old earth must borrow its mirth,
  It has troubles enough of its own.

Sing and the hills will answer,
  Sigh, it is lost on the air,
The echoes bound to a joyful sound
  But shrink from voicing care.

Be glad and your friends are many;
  Be sad and you lose them all,
There are none to decline your nectared wine,
  But alone we must drink life's gall.

There is room in the halls of pleasure
  For a long and lordly train,
But one by one we must all file out
  Through the narrow aisles of pain.

Feast and your halls are crowded,
  Fast and the world goes by,
Succeed and give, 'twill help you live
  But no one can help you die.

Rejoice and men will seek you,
  Grieve and they turn and go;
They want full measure of all your pleasure,
  But they do not want your woe!

Happiness is not in strength, or wealth, or power, or all three.
It lies in ourselves, in true freedom, in the conquest of every
ignoble fear, in perfect self-government, in a power of content-
ment and peace, and the even flow of life, even in poverty, exile,
disease, and the very valley of the shadow of death.

—EPICTETUS.

INVICTUS

WILLIAM ERNEST HENLEY

Out of the night that covers me,
Black as the pit from pole to pole;
I thank whatever gods may be
For my unconquerable soul.

In the fell clutch of circumstance,
I have not winced nor cried aloud;
Beneath the bludgeonings of chance
My head is bloody but unbowed.

Beyond this vale of wrath and tears,
Looms out the horror of the shade;
And yet the menace of the years
Finds, and shall find me, unafraid.

It matters not how strait the gate,
How charged with punishment the scroll;
I am the Master of my fate;
I am the Captain of my soul.

*   *   *   *   *

Seek not to know what must not be revealed;
Joys only flow where Fate is most concealed.
Too-busy man would find his sorrows more
If future fortunes he should know before;
For by that knowledge of his Destiny
He would not live at all, but always die.

Indian Queen, JOHN DRYDEN

SONNET from DIVINE POEMS

by John Donne
The "Poets' Poet"

Death, be not proud, though some have called thee
Mighty and dreadful, for thou are not so;
For those whom thou think'st thou dost overthrow
Die not, poor Death, nor yet canst thou kill me.
From rest and sleep, which but thy pictures be
Much pleasure, then from thee much more must flow;
And soonest our best men with thee do go —
Rest of their bones and souls' delivery!
Thou'rt slave to fate, chance, kings, and desperate men,
And dost with poison, war, and sickness dwell;
And poppy or charms can make us sleep as well,
And better than thy stroke. Why swell'st thou then?
One short sleep past, we wake eternally,
And Death shall be no more: Death, thou shalt die.

Death is the crown of life:
Were death denied, poor man would live in vain;
Were death denied, to live would not be life;
Were death denied, e'en fools would wish to die.
Night Thoughts, Edward Young

Cowards die many times before their deaths;
The valiant never taste of death but once.
Of all the wonders that I yet have heard,
It seems to me most strange that men should fear;
Seeing that death, a necessary end,
Will come when it will come.
Julius Caesar, Act II Scene II, William Shakespeare

CASABIANCA

by Felicia Hemans

[*Young Casabianca, a boy about thirteen years old, son of the Admiral of the Orient, remained at his post (in the Battle of the Nile) after the ship had taken fire and all the guns had been abandoned, and perished in the explosion of the vessel, when the flames had reached the powder.*]

The boy stood on the burning deck,
    Whence all but him had fled;
The flame that lit the battle's wreck
    Shone round him o'er the dead.

Yet beautiful and bright he stood,
    As born to rule the storm;
A creature of heroic blood,
    A proud though childlike form.

The flames rolled on; he would not go
    Without his father's word;
That father, faint in death below,
    His voice no longer heard.

He called aloud, "Say, father, say,
    If yet my task is done!"
He knew not that the chieftain lay
    Unconscious of his son.

"Speak, father!" once again he cried,
    "If I may yet be gone!"
And but the booming shots replied,
    And fast the flames rolled on.

CASABIANCA *(Contd.)*

Upon his brow he felt their breath,
  And in his waving hair,
And looked from that lone post of death
  In still yet brave despair;

And shouted but once more aloud,
  "My father! must I stay?"
While o'er him fast, through sail and shroud,
  The wreathing fires made way.

They wrapt the ship in splendor wild,
  They caught the flag on high,
And streamed above the gallant child,
  Like banners in the sky.

There came a burst of thunder sound;
  The boy, – Oh! where was *he!*
Ask of the winds, that far around
  With fragments strewed the sea, –

With shroud and mast and pennon fair,
  That well had borne their part,–
But the noblest thing that perished there
  Was that young, faithful heart.

Sea-Fever

From SALT-WATER POEMS AND BALLADS
by JOHN MASEFIELD

Reprinted by permission of The Macmillan Company, N.Y.

I MUST go down to the seas again, to the lonely
sea and the sky,
And all I ask is a tall ship and a star to steer her
by,
And the wheel's kick and the wind's song and the
white sail's shaking,
And a grey mist on the sea's face and a grey dawn
breaking.

I must go down to the seas again, for the call of
the running tide
Is a wild call and a clear call that may not be
denied;
And all I ask is a windy day with the white clouds
flying,
And the flung spray and the blown spume, and
the sea-gulls crying.

I must go down to the seas again to the vagrant
gypsy life,
To the gull's way and the whale's way where the
wind's like a whetted knife;
And all I ask is a merry yarn from a laughing
fellow-rover,
And quiet sleep and a sweet dream when the long
trick's over.

(Excerpt From)

THE BALLAD OF EAST AND WEST

by RUDYARD KIPLING

So thou must eat the White Queen's meat, and all her
    foes are thine,
And thou must harry thy father's hold for the peace of
    the Border-line,
And thou must make a trooper tough and hack thy way
    to power—
Belike they will raise thee to Ressaldar when I am
    hanged in Peshawur."
They have looked each other between the eyes, and
    there they found no fault,
They have taken the Oath of the Brother-in-Blood on
    leavened bread and salt:
They have taken the Oath of the Brother-in-Blood on
    fire and fresh cut sod,
On the hilt and the haft of the Khyber knife, and the
    Wondrous Names of God.
The Colonel's son he rides the mare and Kamal's boy
    the dun,
And two have come back to Fort Bukloh where there
    went forth but one.
And when they drew to the Quarter-Guard, full twenty
    swords flew clear—
There was not a man but carried his feud with the blood
    of the mountaineer.
"Ha' done! ha' done!" said the Colonel's son. "Put up
    the steel at your sides!
Last night ye had struck at a Border thief—to-night
    'tis a man of the Guides."

       *   *   *   *   *

Oh, East is East, and West is West, and never the two
    shall meet,
Till Earth and Sky stand presently at God's great
    Judgment Seat;
But there is neither East nor West, Border, nor Breed,
    nor Birth,
When two strong men stand face to face, tho' they come
    from the ends of the earth.

"THE BEAUTY OF HOLINESS"

*An expression by Sidney Lanier of his
passion for truth and sincerity*

"CAN NOT one say with authority to the young artist, whether working in stone, in color, in tones, or in character-forms of the novel: So far from dreading that your moral purpose will interfere with your beautiful creation, go forward in the clear conviction that unless you are suffused— soul and body, one might say — with that moral purpose which finds its largest expression in love; that is, the love of all things in their proper relation; unless you are suffused with this love, do not dare to meddle with beauty; unless you are suffused with beauty, do not dare to meddle with love; unless you are suffused with truth, do not dare to meddle with goodness; in a word, unless you are suffused with truth, wisdom, goodness, and love, abandon the hope that the ages will accept you as an artist."

We are born with faculties and powers capable of almost anything, such as at least would carry us further than can be easily imagined; but it is only the exercise of those powers which gives us ability and skill in anything, and leads us towards perfection.

—JOHN LOCKE.

THE INEVITABLE

by
SARAH KNOWLES BOLTON

I LIKE the man who faces what he must
With step triumphant and a heart of cheer;
Who fights the daily battle without fear;
Sees his hopes fail, yet keeps unfaltering trust
That God is God,—that somehow, true and just
His plans work out for mortals; not a tear
Is shed when fortune, which the world holds dear,
Falls from his grasp—better, with love, a crust
Than living in dishonor; envies not,
Nor loses faith in man; but does his best,
Nor ever murmurs at his humbler lot;
But, with a smile and words of hope, gives zest
To every toiler. He alone is great
Who by a life heroic conquers fate.

If thou faint in the day of thy adversity
thy strength is small
—Proverbs **XXIV**, 10

Adversity is the first path to truth;
He who hath proved war, storm, or
woman's rage,
Whether his winters be eighteen or
eighty,
Has won the experience which is deemed
So weighty.
—Don Juan, **LORD BYRON**

American Aristocracy

by JOHN G. SAXE

*From Library of
Poetry and Song*

by WILLIAM CULLEN BRYANT

OF all the notable things on earth,
The queerest one is pride of birth
    Among our "fierce democracy"!
A bridge across a hundred years,
Without a prop to save it from sneers,
Not even a couple of rotten *peers,*—
A thing for laughter, fleers, and jeers,
    Is American aristocracy!

English and Irish, French and Spanish,
Germans, Italians, Dutch and Danish,
Crossing their veins until they vanish
    In one conglomeration!
So subtle a tangle of blood, indeed,
No Heraldry Harvey will ever succeed
    In finding the circulation.

Depend upon it, my snobbish friend,
Your family thread you can't ascend,
Without good reason to apprehend
You may find it *waxed,* at the farther end,
    By some plebeian vocation!
Or, worse that that, your boasted line
May end in a loop of stronger twine,
    That plagued some worthy relation!

"JUST LIKE GRANDPA"
FROM *THE OLD MAN*

by JAMES WHITCOMB RILEY

Born at Greenfield, Indiana, in 1854, he was a well known writer of poems, prose, and dialect. Most of his writings told of life in his native state at the beginning of this century.

MARK LEMON must have intimately known and loved the genteel old man of the city when the once famous domestic drama of "Grandfather Whitehead" was conceived. In the play the old man—a once prosperous merchant—finds a happy home in the household of his son-in-law. And here it is that the gentle author has drawn at once the poem, the picture, and the living proof of the old Wordsworthian axiom, "The child is father to the man." The old man, in his simple way, and in his great love for his wilful little grandchild, is being continually distracted from the grave sermons and moral lessons he would read the boy. As, for instance, aggrievedly attacking the little fellow's neglect of his books and his inordinate tendency toward idleness and play—the culprit, in the meantime, down on the floor clumsily winding his top—the old man runs on something in this wise:

"Play! play! play! Always play and no work, no study, no lessons. And here you are, the only child of the most indulgent parents in the world—parents that, proud as they are of you, would be ten times prouder only to see you at your book, storing your mind with useful knowledge, instead of, day in, day out, frittering away your time over your toys and your tops and marbles. And even when your old grandfather tries to advise you and wants to help you, and is

The present joys of life we doubly taste by looking back with pleasure on the past.

MARTIAL—*Latin*

What is man? A foolish baby;
Vainly strives, and fights, and frets:
Demanding all, deserving nothing,
One small grave is all he gets.
—*Cui Bono,* THOMAS CARLYLE

always ready and eager to assist you, and all—why, what's it all amount to? Coax and beg and tease and plead with you, and yet—and yet"— (Mechanically kneeling as he speaks) "Now that's not the way to wind your top! How many more times will I have to show you!" And an instant later the old man's admonitions are entirely forgotten, and his artless nature—dull now to everything but the childish glee in which he shares—is all the sweeter and more lovable for its simplicity.

And so it is, Old Man, that you are always touching the very tenderest places in our hearts—unconsciously appealing to our warmest sympathies, and taking to yourself our purest love. We look upon your drooping figure, and we mark your tottering step and trembling hand, yet a reliant something in your face forbids compassion, and a something in your eye will not permit us to look sorrowfully on you. And, however we may smile at your quaint ways and old-school oddities of manner and of speech, our merriment is ever tempered with the gentlest reverence.

Man to the last is but a froward child;
So eager for the future, come what may,
And to the present so insensible.
—*Reflections,* ROGERS

TO MY DOG

by
HENRY DIERKES

I am a king and you, my slave,
My jester and my counsellor;—
To you am I Zeus,
My strength is that of Zethus,
And my song is like to Amphion's,
Else why do you worship me?
Why do you serve me?

Lie down! Sit up!
Come here!
Now go away!

FOR GEORGE GORDON

by
HENRY DIERKES

This is my dream and my desire:
To read my works
Beneath the shaded colonade at Olympia,
With Byron, his distorted limb
Lost in the mist and halo of his
Sainted mind,
Upon my right hand to tell me
When and how I fail;
And on my left . . . a cur,
To praise me with his patient eyes
And gently moving tail.

NO MAN APOLOGIZES FOR DOING RIGHT

by ROBERT BURDETTE

So YOU are not going to church this morning, my son? Ah yes,– I see "the music is not good." That's a pity; that's what we go to church for, to hear the music. And the less we pay, the better music we demand. "And the pews are not comfortable." That's too bad; the Sabbath is a day of rest, and we go to church for repose. The less work we do during the week, the more rest we clamor for on Sunday. "The church is so far away, it's too far to walk and you detest riding your bike when you're all dressed up." This is indeed distressing; sometimes when I think how much farther away Heaven is than the church, and that there are no conveyances on the road, of any description, I wonder how some of us are going to get there. "And the sermon is so long, always." All these things are indeed to be regretted.

I would regret them more sincerely, my boy, did I not know that in a few weeks after the frost is out of the ground, you will squeeze into a hot stuffy car loaded far beyond its stated capacity and ride twenty-miles in miserable traffic, then pay a dollar and a quarter for the privilege of sitting on a hard seat in the broiling sun for three hours watching the local heroes perform at the ball park. Ah, my boy, you see what staying away from church does? It develops a habit of lying. There isn't one man in a hundred who would go on the witness stand and give under oath the same reasons for not going to church that he gives his family every Sunday morning. My son, if you didn't think you ought to go, you wouldn't make any excuses for not going. No man apologizes for doing right.

Judge Joseph Story Speaks...

Joseph Story served as Associate Justice of the United States Supreme Court from 1811 to 1845. His opinions helped to form the basis of later decisions of American courts.

IN OUR future commentaries upon the constitution we shall treat it, then, as it is denominated in the instrument itself, as a constitution of government, ordained and established by the people of the United States for themselves and their posterity. They have declared it the supreme law of the land. They have made it a limited government. They have defined its authority. They have restrained it to the exercise of certain powers, and reserved all others to the states or to the people. It is a popular government. Those who administer it are responsible to the people. It is as popular and just as much emanating from the people as the state governments. It is created for one purpose; the state governments for another. It may be altered, and amended, and abolished at the will of the people. In short, it was made by the people, made for the people, and is responsible to the people.

The constitution of the United States is to receive a reasonable interpretation of its language, and its powers, keeping in view the objects and purposes for which those powers were conferred. By a reasonable interpretation, we mean that in case the words are susceptible of two different senses, the one strict, the other more enlarged, that should be adopted which is most consonant with the apparent objects and intent of the constitution; that which will give it efficacy and force as a *government*, rather than that which will impair its operations and reduce it to a state of imbecility. Of course, we do not mean that the words for this purpose are to be strained beyond their common and natural sense, but keeping within that limit, the exposition is to have a fair and just latitude so as on the one hand to avoid obvious mischief, and on the other hand to promote the public good.

The American Constitution is the most wonderful work ever performed at a given time by the brain and purpose of man.

Gladstone

A Curiosity

Cling to the Mighty One,
Ps. LXXXIX:19

Cling in thy grief;
Heb. XII:11

Cling to the Holy One,
Heb. VII:11

He gives relief;
Ps. CXVI:6

Cling to the Gracious One,
Ps. CXVI:5

Cling in thy pain;
Ps. IV:4

Cling to the Faithful One,
1 Thess. V:25

He will sustain.
Ps. IV:24

Cling to the Living One,
Heb. VII:25

Cling in thy woe.
Ps. LXXXVI:7

Cling to the Living One
1 John IV:16

Through all below;
Rom. VII:38, 39

Cling to the Pardoning One,
John XIV:27

He speaketh peace;
John XIV:23

Cling to the Healing One,
Exod. XV:25

Anguish shall cease.
Ps. CXVII:2

Cling to the Bleeding One,
1 John II:27

Cling to His side
John XX:27

Cling to the Risen One,
Rom. VI:9

In Him abide;
John XV:4

Cling to the Coming One,
Rev. XXII:20

Hope shall arise;
Titus II:13

Cling to the Reigning One,
Ps. XCVII:1

Joy lights thine eyes.
Ps. XVI:11

A MOST UNUSUAL WILL

Originally Filed in the
Probate Court of Cook County, Illinois

I, being of sound and disposing mind and memory, do hereby make and publish this my last will and testament in order as to justly as may be, to distribute my interest in the world among succeeding men.

That part of my interest which is known in law and recognized in the sheep-bound volumes as my property, being inconsiderable and of no account, I make no disposition of in this, my will. My right to live, being but a life estate, is not at my disposal, but, these things excepted, all else in the world I now proceed to devise and bequeath.

Item: I give to good fathers and mothers, in trust for their children, all good little words of praise and encouragement, and all quaint pet names and endearment; and I charge said parents to use them justly, but generously, as the deeds of their children shall require.

Item: I leave to children inclusively, but only for the term of their childhood, all and every flower of the field and the blossoms of the woods, with the right to play among them freely according to the custom of children, warning them at the same time against thistles and thorns. And I devise to children the banks of the brooks and the golden sands beneath the waters thereof, and the odors of the willows that dip therein, and the white clouds that float high over giant trees. And I leave the children the long, long days to be

Do noble things, not dream them, all day long;
And so make life, death, and that vast forever
One grand, sweet song.

—A Farewell, CHARLES KINGSLEY

merry in, in a thousand ways, and the night and the train of the Milky Way to wonder at, but subject, nevertheless to the rights hereinafter given to lovers.

Item: I devise to boys, jointly, all the useful idle fields and commons where ball may be played, all pleasant waters where one may swim, all snow-clad hills where one may coast, and all streams and ponds where one may fish, or where, when grim winter comes, one may skate, to hold the same for the period of their boyhood. And all meadows with the clover-blossoms and butterflies thereof; the woods with their beauty; the squirrels and the birds and the echoes and strange noises, and all distant places, which may be visited, together with the adventures there found. And I give to said boys each his own place at the fireside at night, with all pictures that may be seen in the burning wood, to enjoy without let or hindrance or without any encumbrance or care.

Item: To lovers I devise their imaginary world, with whatever they may need, as the stars of the sky, the red roses by the wall, the bloom of the hawthorn, the sweet strains of music, and aught else they may desire to figure to each other the lastingness and beauty of their love.

Item: To young men jointly I bequeath all the boisterous, inspiring sports of rivalry, and I give to them the disdain of weakness, and undaunted confidence in their own strength. Tho they are rude, I leave to them the power to make lasting friendships, and of possessing companions, and to them,

Man is a noble animal, splendid in ashes
and pompous in the grave.
        —Urn Burial, SIR THOMAS BROWNE

exclusively, I give all merry songs and grave choruses to sing with lusty voices.

Item: And to those who are no longer children or youths or lovers, I leave memory; and bequeath to them the volumes of the poems of Burns and Shakespeare and of other poets, if there be others, to the end that they may live in the old days over again, freely and fully without tithe or diminution.

Item: To our loved ones with snowy crowns, I bequeath the happiness of old age, the love and gratitude of their children until they fall asleep.

In thy lone and long night-watches, sky
above and sea below,
Thou didst learn a higher wisdom than
the babbling schoolmen know;
God's stars and silence taught thee, as
his angels only can,
That the one sole sacred thing beneath
the cope of heaven is man.
—*The Branded Hand,* JOHN GREENLEAF WHITTIER

There was a flower called *Faith*:
Man plucked it, and kept it in a vase of water.
This was long ago mark you.
And the flower is now faint,
For the water with time and dust is foul.
Come let us pour out the old water,
and put in new,
That the flower of *Faith* may be red again.

From Poem Outlines by Sidney Lanier

FROM
IN MEMORIAM

ALFRED LORD TENNYSON

Ring out, wild bells, to the wild sky,
  The flying cloud, the frosty light:
  The year is dying in the night;
Ring out, wild bells, and let him die.

Ring out the old, ring in the new,
  Ring happy bells, across the snow:
  The year is going, let him go;
Ring out the false, ring in the true.

Ring out the grief that snaps the mind,
  For those that here we see no more;
  Ring out the feud of rich and poor,
Ring in redress to all mankind.

Ring out a slowly dying cause,
  And ancient forms of party strife;
  Ring in the nobler modes of life,
With sweeter manners, purer laws.

Ring out the want, the care, the sin,
  The faithless coldness of the times;
  Ring out, ring out my mournful rhymes,
But ring the fuller minstrel in.

Ring out false pride in place and blood,
  The civic slander and the spite;
  Ring in the love of truth and right,
Ring in the common love of good.

The noblest motive is the public good. —VIRGIL

A RECEIPT FOR SALAD
SIDNEY SMITH

To make this condiment your poet begs
The pounded yellow of two hard-boiled eggs;
Two boiled potatoes, passed through kitchen sieve,
Smoothness and softness to the salad give;
Let onion atoms lurk within the bowl,
And, half suspected, animate the whole;
Of mordent mustard add a single spoon,
Distrust the condiment that bites so soon;
But deem it not, thou man of herbs, a fault
To add a double quantity of salt;
Four times the spoon with oil from Lucca crown,
And twice with vinegar, procured from town;
And lastly, o'er the flavored compound toss
A magic soupcon of anchovy sauce.
O green and glorious! O herbaceous treat!
'T would tempt the dying anchorite to eat;
Back to the world he'd turn his fleeting soul,
And plunge his fingers in the salad bowl;
Serenely full, the epicure would say,
"Fate cannot harm me,—I have dined to-day."

THE PEDLER'S PACK
From "THE WINTERS TALE"
WILLIAM SHAKESPEARE

Lawn as white as driven snow;
Cyprus black as e'er was crow;
Gloves as sweet as damask roses;
Masks for faces and for noses;
Bugle bracelet, necklace-amber,
Perfume for a lady's chamber:
Golden quoifs and stomachers,
For my lads to give their dears;
Pins and poking sticks of steel,
What maids lack from head to heel:
Come buy of me, come; come buy, come buy;
Buy, lads, or else your lasses cry:
Come buy.

DEEP

by HENRY DIERKES
From *The Man From Vermont*
Eileen Baskerville, Oak Park, Illinois, Publisher

You did not come today.
It is the first Sunday since I have been here
That I have not heard your step
Upon the gravel.
Once ... quite late ...
I thought I heard you,
But it was the fair-haired girl
Whose father lies close by.
She comes on Wednesdays and Sundays.
I'm sure she makes him happy.

She stopped today and looked down upon me,
Because it says upon my stone
That I have given my life for something,
Something she cannot quite understand.
My epitaph is far too ornamental in its
Wording;
I should have liked it simpler:
"... who could not die
Because he did not live ..."
That would start the grey-haired ones
Scratching their soft scalps.
It might even stop the professional chap
Who twice a month
Brings peonies to lay upon his sister's grave.
I'd rather like to have *him* look at me
And think a little.

* * * * *

'Tis the divinity that stirs within us;
'Tis heaven itself that points out an hereafter,
And intimates eternity to man.
Eternity! thou pleasing, dreadful thought!

Cato, JOSEPH ADDISON

You did not come today, but then...
The sky was clear
And the sun warmed everything in brightness,
Perhaps you——
But you will come next Sunday.

Do you remember, how,
When I had fallen asleep over a book
And the night air chilled through
The open windows,
You used to tiptoe in
With the white shawl grandmother made;
How you'd tuck it about me
And then go away after kissing my forehead?
(I was almost always awake,
But it might have made you a little less
Gentle in your touch,
Had you not thought you might disturb me.)

On a Sunday when it is cold and cheerless,
Bring the white shawl with you and lay it
Over me.
It will lie close about me,
Covering the grass and the random weeds,
And I shall be warm.
And then... if you'd put your lips
Upon a leaf of the little rosebush
You planted for me early in the summer,
(a gentle kiss, because you fear to waken me)
I'd know that you had kissed my forehead.

Then I could die.

It is but crossing with a bated breath,
A white, set face, a little strip of sea—
To find the loved one waiting on the shore,
More beautiful, more precious than before.

ELLA WHEELER WILCOX

Contentment

OLIVER WENDELL HOLMES

LITTLE I ask; my wants are few;
  I only wish a hut of stone,
(A *very plain* brown stone will do,)
  That I may call my own;
And close at hand is such a one,
In yonder street that fronts the sun.

Plain food is quite enough for me;
  Three courses are as good as ten;—
If nature can subsist on three,
  Thank Heaven for three. Amen!
I always thought cold victual nice;—
My *choice* would be vanilla-ice.

I care not much for gold or land;—
  Give me a mortgage here and there,—
Some good bank-stock,— some note of hand,
  Or trifling railroad share,—
I only ask that Fortune send
A *little* more than I shall spend.

Honors are silly toys, I know,
  And titles are but empty names;
I would, *perhaps,* be Plenipo,—
  But only near St. James;
I'm very sure I should not care
To fill our Gubernator's chair.

Jewels are bawbles; 't is a sin
  To care for such unfruitful things;—
Our good-sized diamond in a pin,—
  Some, *not so large,* in rings,—
A ruby, and a pearl or so,
Will do for me;— I laugh at show.

My dame should dress in cheap attire:
    (Good heavy silks are never dear;) –
I own perhaps I *might* desire
    Some shawls of true Cashmere, –
Some marrowy crapes of China silk,
Like wrinkled skins on scalded milk.

I would not have the horse I drive
    So fast that folks must stop and stare;
An easy gait, – two, forty-five, –
    Suits me; I do not care; –
Perhaps, for just a *single spurt*,
Some seconds less would do no hurt.

Of pictures, I should like to own
    Titians and Raphaels three or four, –
I love so much their style and tone, –
    One Turner, and no more,
(A landscape, – foreground golden dirt, –
The sunshine painted with a squirt.)

Of books but few, – some fifty score
    For daily use, and bound for wear;
The rest upon an upper floor; –
    Some *little* luxury *there*
Of red morocco's gilded gleam,
And vellum rich as country cream.

That two men may be real friends, they must have opposite opinions, similar principles, and different loves and hatreds.

Chateaubriand

A PSALM OF LIFE

by

HENRY WADSWORTH LONGFELLOW

What the heart of the young man said to the Psalmist

Tell me not, in mournful numbers,
    Life is but an empty dream!—
For the soul is dead that slumbers,
    And things are not what they seem.

Life is real! Life is earnest!
    And the grave is not its goal;
Dust thou art, to dust returnest,
    Was not spoken of the soul.

Not enjoyment, and not sorrow,
    Is our destined end or way;
But to act, that each tomorrow
    Find us farther than today.

Art is long, and Time is fleeting,
    And our hearts, though stout and brave,
Still, like muffled drums, are beating
    Funeral marches to the grave.

In the world's broad field of battle,
    In the bivouac of Life,
Be not like dumb, driven cattle!
    Be a hero in the strife!

*For what is your life? It is even a vapor, that appeareth for a
little time, and then vanisheth away.*

                                                    JAMES IV:14

Page One Hundred Seventy Six

Trust no Future, howe'er pleasant!
  Let the dead Past bury its dead!
Act,—act in the living Present!
  Heart within, and God o'erhead!

Lives of great men all remind us
  We can make our lives sublime,
And, departing, leave behind us
  Footprints on the sands of time;

Footprints, that perhaps another,
  Sailing o'er life's solemn main,
A forlorn and shipwrecked brother,
  Seeing, shall take heart again.

Let us then, be up and doing,
  With a heart for any fate;
Still achieving, still pursuing,
  Learn to labor and to wait.

*   *   *   *   *

*In the sweat of thy face shalt thou eat bread, till thou
return unto the ground; for out of it wast thou taken.*
                              GENESIS III:19

*No man is born into the world whose work
Is not born with him. There is always work,
And tools to work withal, for those who will;
And blessed are the horny hands of toil.*
                    A Glance Behind the Curtain,
                          JAMES RUSSELL LOWELL

*Our grand business undoubtedly is,
not to see what lies dimly at a distance,
but to do what lies clearly at hand.*
        Essays: Signs of the Times, THOMAS CARLYLE

THE EMPTY CRIB

by

ELEEN DHU

Last night I lay with dry and staring eyes,
   And ears that listened for some dreadful sound
And often, yielding to an urge to rise,
   I leaned above a little bed of white
   Where some pale finger of the moon's far light
   Had found my son's soft hair so golden bright
It shed a gentle halo all around.

And thus it is with mothers through this land;
   They can but rise to burn a vigil light;
On weary, willing feet they can but stand,
   Well knowing there will be no hour of sleep
   For one small mother, who must strangely keep
   A fearful watch in grief that lies too deep
For tears;—a crib stands empty in the night!

(O Mater Dolorosa, take her hand;
You lived, and bore it all; you understand.)

* * * * *

*But Jesus said, Suffer little children and forbid them
not to come unto me for of such is the kingdom of
heaven.*

MATTHEW XIX:14

* * * * *

*Children sweeten labors, but they make misfortunes
more bitter: they increase the cares of life, but they
mitigate the remembrance of death.*

Of Parents and Children, SIR FRANCIS BACON

"Youth I Do Adore Thee"

FROM

The Passionate Pilgrim by BARNARD

Crabbed age and youth cannot live together;
Youth is full of pleasure, age is full of care;
Youth like summer morn, age like winter weather;
Youth like summer brave, age like winter bare.
Youth is full of sport, age's breath is short;
Youth is nimble, age is lame;
Youth is hot and bold, age is weak and cold;
Youth is wild, and age is tame.
Age, I do abhor thee; youth I do adore thee.

Rejoice, O young man in thy youth.
ECCLESIASTES XI:9

Remember now thy Creator in the days of thy youth.
ECCLESIASTES XII:1

There still are many rainbows in your sky,
  But mine are vanish'd. All, when life is new,
Commence with feelings warm and prospects high,
  But time strips our illusions of their hue.
Don Juan, LORD BYRON

Gather the rose-buds while ye may,
  Old time is still a-flying,
And that same flower that blooms today,
  Tomorrow shall by dying.
The Seasons, JAMES THOMSON

"VAIN POMP AND GLORY
OF THIS WORLD, I HATE YE"

From HENRY VIII, SCENE II

WILLIAM SHAKESPEARE

THIS is the state of man: today he puts forth
The tender leaves of hopes; tomorrow blossoms,
And bears his blushing honors thick upon him;
The third day comes a frost, a killing frost;
And, when he thinks, good easy man, full surely
His greatness is a-ripening, nips his root,
And then he falls, as I do. I have ventur'd
Like little wanton boys that swim on bladders,
This many summers in a sea of glory,
But far beyond my depth: my high-blown pride
At length broke under me, and now has left me,
Weary and old with service, to the mercy
Of a rude stream, that must forever hide me.
Vain pomp and glory of this world, I hate ye:
I feel my heart new open'd. O! how wretched
Is that poor man that hangs on princes' favors!
There is, betwixt that smile we would aspire to,
That sweet aspect of princes, and their ruin,
More pangs and fears than wars or women have;
And when he falls, he falls like Lucifer,
Never to hope again.

Brutes find out where their talents lie:
A bear will not attempt to fly
A founder'd horse will oft debate,
Before he tries a five-barr'd gate;
A dog by instinct turns aside,
Who sees the ditch too deep and wide;
But men we find the only creature
Who, led by folly, combats nature;
Who when she loudly cries—forbear,
With obstinacy fixes there;
And, where his genius least inclines,
Absurdly bends his whole designs.

On Poetry, JONATHAN SWIFT

Art Thou Weary?

(825-794)

From The World's Great Catholic Poetry, WALSH

From the Greek, by J. M. Neale
Reprinted by permission of The Macmillan Company, N. Y.

Art thou weary, art thou languid,
　Art thou sore distrest?
"Come to me," saith One, "and coming,
　Be at rest!"
Hath He marks to lead me to Him
　If He be my Guide?
"In His Feet and Hands are Wound-prints,
　And His side."
Is there Diadem, as Monarch,
　That His Brow adorns?
"Yea, a Crown, in very surety,
　But of Thorns!"
If I find Him, if I follow,
　What His guerdon here?
"Many a sorrow, many a labor,
　Many a tear."
If I still hold closely to Him,
　What hath He at last?
"Sorrow vanquished, labor ended,
If I ask Him to receive me,
　Will He say me nay?
"Not till earth and not till heaven
　Pass away!"
Finding, following, keeping, struggling,
　Is He sure to bless?
"Angels, Martyrs, Prophets, Virgins,
　Answer, Yes!"

FIRST CHAPTER

THE ADVENTURES OF

HUCKLEBERRY FINN

By MARK TWAIN

A Masterpiece of Description

YOU don't know about me without you have read a book by the name of *The Adventures of Tom Sawyer;* but that ain't no matter. That book was made by Mr. Mark Twain, and he told the truth, mainly. There was things which he stretched, but mainly he told the truth. That is nothing. I never seen anybody but lied one time or another, without it was Aunt Polly, or the widow, or maybe Mary. Aunt Polly—Tom's Aunt Polly, she is—and Mary, and the Widow Douglas is all told about in that book, which is mostly a true book, with some stretchers, as I said before.

Now the way that the book winds up is this: Tom and me found the money that the robbers hid in the cave, and it made us rich. We got six thousand dollars apiece—all gold. It was an awful sight of money when it was piled up. Well, Judge Thatcher he took it and put it out at interest, and it fetched us a dollar a day apiece all the year round—more than a body could tell what to do with. The Widow Douglas she took me for her son, and allowed she would sivilize me; but it was rough living in the house all the time, considering how dismal regular and decent the widow was in all her ways; and so when I couldn't stand it no longer I lit out. I got into my old rags and my sugar-hogshead again, and was free and satisfied. But Tom Sawyer he hunted me up and said he was going to start a band of robbers, and I might join if I would go back to the widow and be respectable. So I went back.

The widow she cried over me, and called me a poor lost lamb, and she called me a lot of other names, too, but she never meant no harm by it. She put me in them new clothes again, and I couldn't do nothing but sweat and sweat, and feel all cramped up. Well, then, the old thing commenced again. The widow rung a bell for supper, and you had to come to time. When you got to the table you couldn't go right to eating, but you had to wait for the widow to tuck down her head and grumble a little over the victuals, though there warn't really anything the matter with them,—that is, nothing, only everything was cooked by itself. In a barrel of odds and ends it is different; things get mixed up, and the juice kind of swaps around, and the things go better.

After supper she got out her book and she learned me about Moses and the Bulrushers, and I was in a sweat to find out all about him; but by-and-by she let it out that Moses had been dead a considerable long time; so then I didn't care no more about him, because I don't take no stock in dead people.

Pretty soon I wanted to smoke, and asked the widow to let me. But she wouldn't. She said it was a mean practice and wasn't clean, and I must try to not do it any more. That is just the way with some people. They get down on a thing when they don't know nothing about it. Here she was a-bothering about Moses, which was no kin to her, and no use to anybody, being gone, you see, yet finding a power of fault with me for doing a thing that had some good in it. And she took snuff, too; of course that was all right, because she done it herself.

Her sister, Miss Watson, a tolerable slim old maid, with goggles on, had just come to live with her, and took a set at me now with a spelling-book. She worked me middling hard for about an hour, and then the widow made her ease up. I couldn't stood it much longer. Then for an hour it was deadly dull, and I was fidgety. Miss Watson would say, "Don't put your feet up there, Huckleberry;" and "Don't scrunch up like that, Huckleberry – set up straight;" and pretty soon she would say, "Don't gap and stretch like that, Huckleberry – why don't you try to behave?" Then she told me all about the bad place, and I said I wished I was there. She got mad then, but I didn't mean no harm. All I wanted was to go somewheres; all I wanted was a change, I warn't particular. She said it was wicked to say what I said; said she wouldn't say it for the whole world; *she* was going to live so as to go to the good place. Well, I couldn't see no advantage in going where she was going, so I made up my mind I wouldn't try for it. But I never said so, because it would only make trouble, and wouldn't do no good.

Now she had got a start, and she went on and told me all about the good place. She said all a body would have to do there was to go around all day long with a harp and sing, for ever and ever. So I didn't think much of it. But I never said so. I asked her if she reckoned Tom Sawyer would go there, and she said not by a considerable sight. I was glad about that, because I wanted him and me to be together.

Miss Watson she kept pecking at me, and it got tiresome and lonesome. By-and-by they fetched the Negroes in and had prayers, and then everybody was off to bed. I went up to my room with a piece of candle, and put it on the table. Then I set down in a chair by the window and tried to think of something cheerful, but it warn't no use. I felt so lonesome I most wished I was dead. The stars were shining, and the leaves rustled in the woods ever so mournful; and I heard an owl, away off, who-whooing about somebody that was dead, and a whippowill and a dog crying about somebody that was going to die; and the wind was trying to whisper something to me, and I couldn't make out what it was, and so it made the cold shivers run over me. Then away out in the woods I heard that kind of a sound that a ghost makes when it wants to tell about something that's on its mind and can't make itself understood, and so can't rest easy in its grave, and has to go about that way every night grieving. I got so down-hearted and scared I did wish I had some company. Pretty soon a spider went crawling up my shoulder, and I flipped it off and it lit in the candle; and before I could budge it was all shrivelled up. I didn't need anybody to tell me that that was an awful bad sign and would fetch me some bad luck, so I was scared and most shook the clothes off of me. I got up and turned around in my tracks three times and crossed my breast every time; and then I tied up a little lock of my hair with a thread to keep witches away. But I hadn't no confidence. You do that when you've lost a horseshoe that you've found, instead of nailing it up over the door, but I hadn't ever heard anybody say it was any way to keep off bad luck when you'd killed a spider.

I set down again, a-shaking all over, and got out my pipe for a smoke; for the house was all as still as death now, and so the widow wouldn't know. Well, after a long time I heard the clock away off in the town go boom – boom – boom – twelve licks; and all still again – stiller than ever. Pretty soon I heard a twig snap down in the dark amongst the trees – something was a stirring. I set still and listened. Directly I could just barely hear a *"me-yow! me-yow!"* down there. That was good! Says I, *"me-yow! me-yow!"* as soft as I could, and then I put out the light and scrambled out of the window on to the shed. Then I slipped down to the ground and crawled in among the trees, and, sure enough, there was Tom Sawyer waiting for me.

The name of *American* which belongs to you, in your national capacity, must always exalt the just pride of patriotism more than any appellation to be derived from any local discriminations. The independence and liberty you possess are the work of joint councils and joint efforts—of common dangers, sufferings, and successes.

Washington's Farewell Address

TO THE TEACHERS OF AMERICA

by

OLIVER WENDELL HOLMES

T EACHERS of teachers! Yours the task,
Noblest that noble minds can ask,
High up Aonia's murmurous mount,
To watch, to guard the sacred fount
   That feeds the streams below;
To guide the hurrying flood that fills
A thousand silvery rippling rills
   In ever-widening flow.

Rich is the harvest from the fields
That bounteous Nature kindly yields,
But fairer growths enrich the soil
Ploughed deep by thought's unwearied
    toil
   In Learning's broad domain.
And where the leaves, the flowers, the
    fruits,
Without your watering at the roots,
   To fill each branching vein?

Welcome! the Author's firmest friends,
Your voice the surest Godspeed lends.
Of you the growing mind demands
The patient care, the guiding hands,
   Through all the mists of morn.
And knowing well the future's need,
Your prescient wisdom sows the seed
   To flower in years unborn.

A little learning is a dangerous thing;
Drink deep, or taste not, the Pierian spring;
For shallow thoughts intoxicate the brain,
And drinking deeply sobers us again.
        Essay on Criticism, **ALEXANDER POPE**

LOVE-THE KEY TO ACCOMPLISHMENT

Though Sidney Lanier directs his reference to the young artist in this philosophy it applies equally to all —

"CAN NOT one say with authority to the young artist, whether working in stone, in color, in tones, or in character-forms of the novel: So far from dreading that your moral purpose will interfere with your beautiful creation, go forward in the clear conviction that unless you are suffused—soul and body, one might say—with that moral purpose which finds its largest expression in love; that is, the love of all things in their proper relation; unless you are suffused with this love, do not dare to meddle with beauty; unless you are suffused with beauty, do not dare to meddle with love; unless you are suffused with truth, do not dare to meddle with goodness; in a word, unless you are suffused with truth, wisdom, goodness, and love, abandon the hope that the ages will accept you as an artist."

Perfect wisdom hath four parts: wisdom, the principle of doing things right; justice, the principle of doing things equally in public and private; fortitude, the principle of not flying danger, but meeting it; and temperance, the principle of subduing desires, and living moderately.

PLATO

Little Things

WILLA HOEY

It's the little things we do and say
    That mean so much as we go our way.
A kindly deed can lift a load
    From weary shoulders on the road,
Or a gentle word, like summer rain,
    May soothe some heart and banish pain.
What joy or sadness often springs
    From just the simple little things!

The Simple Way

MALCOLM SCHLOSS

Love without ceasing,
    Give without measure—
Who can exhaust
    God's limitless treasure?

VIVID DESCRIPTION

FROM

"A REMARKABLE MAN"

by JAMES WHITCOMB RILEY

THAT NIGHT was a bragging, blustering, bullying sort of a night. The wind was mad—stark, staring mad; running over and around the town, howling and whooping like a maniac. It whirled and whizzed, and wheeled about and whizzed again. It pelted the pedestrian's face with dust that stung like sleet. It wrenched at the signs, and rattled the doors and windows till the lights inside shivered as with affright. The unfurled awnings fluttered and flapped over the deserted streets like monstrous bats or birds of prey; and, gritting their iron teeth, the shutters lunged and snapped at their fastenings convulsively. Such a night as we like to hide away from, and with a good cigar, a good friend, and a good fire, talk of soothing things and dream. My friend and I were not so isolated, however, upon this occasion; for the suddenness of the storm had driven us, for shelter, into "Bowers's Emporium"; and, seated in the rear of the spacious and brightly illuminated store, we might almost "dream we dwelt in marble halls," were it not for the rather profuse display of merchandise and a voluminous complement of show-cards, reading "Bargains in Overcoats," "Best and Cheapest Underwear," "Buy Bowers's Boots!" etc.

Most of us have experienced just such a night, but few have ever put into words such an accurate description.

Selection From
THANATOPSIS

by
WILLIAM CULLEN BRYANT

AS THE long train
Of ages glides away, the sons of men –
The youth in life's fresh spring, and he who goes
In the full strength of years, matron and maid,
The speechless babe, and the gray-headed man –
Shall one by one be gathered to thy side,
By those, who in their turn shall follow them.

So live, that when thy summons comes to join
The innumerable caravan, which moves
To that mysterious realm, where each shall take
His chamber in the silent halls of death,
Thou go not, like the quarry-slave at night,
Scourged to his dungeon, but, sustained and soothed
By an unfaltering trust, approach thy grave
Like one who wraps the drapery of his couch
About him, and lies down to pleasant dreams.

*Reputation is what men and women think of us. Character
is what God and angels know of us.*
                                        —THOMAS PAINE

*How many people live on the reputation of the reputation
they might have made!*
                    The Autocrat of the Breakfast Table
                              OLIVER WENDELL HOLMES

*So live that you would not mind selling your pet parrot
to the town gossip.*
                                        —WILL ROGERS

GOD LEFT THE CHALLENGE
IN THE EARTH

by DR. ALLEN STOCKDALE

By courtesy of NATIONAL ASSOCIATION OF MANUFACTURERS
(Excerpt) reprinted by Permission, PUBLIC AID IN ILLINOIS,
November 1957.

WHEN God made the Earth, He could have finished it.
But He didn't. Instead, He left it as a raw material—to tease
us, to tantalize us, to set us thinking and experimenting and
risking and adventuring! And therein we find our supreme
interest in living.

Have you ever noticed that small children in a nursery
will ignore clever mechanical toys in order to build, with
spools and strings and sticks and blocks, a world of their own
imagination?

And so with grown-ups, too. God gave us a world unfin-
ished, so that we might share in the joys and satisfactions
of creation.

He left the oil in Trenton rock.

He left the electricity in the clouds.

He left the rivers un-bridged—and the mountains un-
trailed.

He left the forests un-felled and the cities un-built.

He left the laboratories un-opened.

He left the diamonds un-cut.

He gave us the challenge of raw materials, not the satisfaction of perfect, finished things.

He left the music un-sung and the dramas un-played.

He left the poetry un-dreamed, in order that men and
women might not become bored, but engage in stimulating,
exciting, creative activities that keep them thinking, working, experimenting, and experiencing all the joys and dur-
able satisfactions of achievement.

A man in Florida turned a miserable old green-water
swamp, mosquito-infested and snake-inhabited, into a beautiful garden.

When we go about our work earnestly and perseveringly, it often happens that although we have to tack about again and again, we get ahead of those who are helped by wind and tide.

—GOETHE

Once a sanctimonious visitor, who was inspecting it, exclaimed "Oh, dear brother, what a beautiful garden you and the Lord have made from that swamp!"

"Yes," came the reply, "but you should have seen it when the Lord had it all by Himself!"

So it is with all the world. There is no Shangri-La where our every want can be supplied by wishing. There is no substance to the philosophy of "getting by." There is nothing worth while gained by chance.

Work, thought, creation. These give life its stimulus, its real satisfaction, its intriguing value.

I am a true laborer;
I earn that I eat,
Get that I wear;
Owe no man hate,
Envy no man's happiness,
Glad of other men's good.

—WILLIAM SHAKESPEARE

MARK ANTONY SPEAKS—

ACT III, SCENE II, JULIUS CAESAR – by WILLIAM SHAKESPEARE
Written in the year 1600

Friends, Romans, countrymen, lend me your ears;
I come to bury Caesar, not to praise him.
The evil that men do lives after them,
The good is oft interred with their bones;
So let it be with Caesar. The noble Brutus
Hath told you Caesar was ambitious;
If it were so, it was a grievous fault,
And grievously hath Caesar answer'd it.
Here, under leave of Brutus and the rest,—
For Brutus is an honourable man;
So are they all, all honourable men,—
Come I to speak in Caesar's funeral.
He was my friend, faithful and just to me:
But Brutus says he was ambitious;
And Brutus is an honourable man.
He hath brought many captives home to Rome,
Whose ransoms did the general coffers fill:
Did this in Caesar seem ambitious?
When that the poor have cried, Caesar hath wept;
Ambition should be made of sterner stuff:
Yet Brutus says he was ambitious;
And Brutus is an honourable man.
You all did see that on the Lupercal
I thrice presented him a kingly crown,
Which he did thrice refuse: was this ambition?
Yet Brutus says he was ambitious;
And, sure, he is an honourable man.
I speak not to disprove what Brutus spoke,
But here I am to speak what I do know.
You all did love him once, not without cause:
What cause withholds you then to mourn for him?
O judgment! thou art fled to brutish beasts,
And men have lost their reason. Bear with me;
My heart is in the coffin there with Caesar,
And I must pause till it come back to me.

ADVICE TO A FRIEND

by PHILIP FRENEAU

Poet of the Revolutionary War

S O LONG harass'd by winds and seas,
'Tis time, a length, to take your ease,
Change ruffian waves for quiet groves
And war's loud blast for sylvan loves.

In all your rounds, 'tis passing strange
No fair one tempts you to a change—
Madness it is, you must agree,
To lodge alone 'till *forty-three.*

Old Plato own'd, no blessing here
Could equal Love—if but sincere;
And writings penn'd by heaven, have shown
That man can ne'er be blest alone.

O'er life's meridian have you pass'd;
The night of death advances fast!
No props you plant for your decline,
No partner sooths these cares of thine.

If Neptune's self, who rul'd the main,
Kept sea-nymphs there to ease his pain;
Yourself, who skim that empire o'er,
May surely have one nymph from shore.—

Myrtilla fair, in yonder grove,
Has so much beauty, so much love,
That, on her lip, the meanest fly
Is happier far than you or I.

Marry your son when you will,
and your daughter when you can.
FRENCH PROVERB

Christmas Thoughts

By the Editors of

C HRISTMAS is celebration; and celebration is instinct in the heart. With gift and feast, with scarlet ribbon and fresh green bough, with merriment and the sound of music, we commend the day — oasis in the long, long landscape of the commonplace. Through how many centuries, through how many threatening circumstances, has Christmas been celebrated since that cry came ringing down the ages, "Fear not: for, behold, I bring you good tidings of great joy, which shall be to all people. For unto you is born this day in the city of David a Saviou , which is Christ the Lord."

Christmas is celebration, but the traditions that cluster sweetly around the day have significance only if they translate the heart's intention — the yearning of the human spirit to compass and express faith and hope and love. Without this intention, the gift is bare, and the celebration a touch of tinsel, and the time without meaning. As these attributes, exemplifying the divine spark in mankind, informed the first Christmas and have survived the onslaughts of relentless time, so do they shine untarnished in this present Year of our Lord.

Faith and hope and love, which cannot be bought or sold or bartered but only given away, are the wellsprings, firm and deep, of Christmas celebration. These are the gifts without price, the ornaments incapable of imitation, discovered only within oneself and therefore unique. They are not always easy to come by, but they are in unlimited supply, ever in the province of all.

Of all the old festivals . . . that of Christmas awakens the strongest and most heartfelt associations. There is a tone of solemn and sacred

For All The Year

McCALL's, *December 1959*

THIS CHRISTMAS, mend a quarrel. Seek out a forgotten friend. Dismiss suspicion, and replace it with trust. Write a love letter. Share some treasure. Give a soft answer. Encourage youth. Manifest your loyalty in word and deed. Keep a promise. Find the time. Forgo a grudge. Forgive an enemy. Listen. Apologize if you were wrong. Try to understand. Flout envy. Examine your demands on others. Think first of someone else. Appreciate. Be kind; be gentle. Laugh a little. Laugh a little more. Deserve confidence. Take up arms against malice. Decry complacency. Express your gratitude. Go to church. Welcome a stranger. Gladden the heart of a child. Take pleasure in the beauty and wonder of the earth. Speak your love. Speak it again. Speak it still once again.

These are but inklings of a vast category; a mere scratching of the surface. They are simple things; you have heard them all before; but their influence has never been measured.

Christmas is celebration, and there is no celebration that compares with the realization of its true meaning—with the sudden stirring of the heart that has extended itself toward the core of life. Then, only then, is it possible to grasp the significance of that first Christmas—to savor in the inward ear the wild, sweet music of the angel choir; to envision the star-struck sky, and glimpse, behind the eyelids, the ray of light that fell athwart a darkened path and changed the world.

feeling that blends with our conviviality and lifts the spirit to a state of hallowed and elevated enjoyment.

—WASHINGTON IRVING
Christmas Papers

JEST 'FORE CHRISTMAS

by

Eugene Field, *newspaperman and poet*
— a Christmas poem that never grows old

Father calls me William, sister calls me Will,
Mother calls me Willie, but the fellers call me Bill!
Mighty glad I a'nt a girl—ruther be a boy.
Without them sashes, curls an' things that's worn by Fauntleroy!
Love to chawnk green apples an' go swimmin' in the lake,
Hate to take the castor ile they give for belly-ache!
Most all the time the whole year round there ain't no flies on me,
But jest 'fore Christmas I'm as good as good kin be!
Got a yeller dog named Sport, sick him on the cat,
First thing she knows, she doesn't know where she is at!
Got a clipper sled, and when us kids goes out to slide,
'Long comes the grocery cart, 'nd we all hook a ride!
But sometimes when the grocery man is worrited an' cross,
He rushes at us with his whip an' larrups up his hoss,
An' then I laff and' holler, "Oh, ye never teched *me!*"
But jest 'fore Christmas I'm good as I kin be!
Gran'ma says she hopes that, when I git to be a man,
I'll be a missionary like her oldest brother, Dan
As was et up by the cannibuls that lives in Clyton's Isle,
Where every prospect pleases an' only man is vile!
But gran'ma she has never been to see a Wild West show
Nor read the life of Daniel Boone, or else I guess she'd know
That Buff'lo Bill an' cowboys is good enough for me—
'Cept jest 'fore Christmas, when I'm good as good kin be!
And then old Sport he hangs around, so solemnlike an' still,
His eyes they seem a-sayin', "What's the matter, little Bill?"
The old cat sneaks down off her perch an' wonders what's become
Of them two enemies of hern that used to make things burn!
But I am *so* polite an' tend so earnestly to biz,
That Mother says to Father: "How improved our Willie is!"
But Father, havin' been a boy hisself, suspicions me
When, jest 'fore Christmas, I'm as good as I kin be!

A DESCRIPTIVE MASTERPIECE

An eyewitness account of the last Indian war dance ever held in what is now the city of Chicago as told by John D. Caton, a former chief justice of the state of Illinois. This scene took place in 1836.

THERE were engaged in the dance probably five hundred braves at least. All were entirely naked except a strip of cloth around the loins. Their bodies were covered all over with a great variety of brilliant paints. On their faces particularly they seemed to have exhausted their art of hideous decoration. Foreheads, cheeks and noses were covered with curved stripes of red or vermillion which were edged with black points, and gave the appearance of a horrid grin over the entire countenance. The long coarse black hair was gathered into scalp locks on the tops of their heads and decorated with a profusion of hawks' and eagles' feathers, some strung together so as to extend down the back nearly to the ground. They were principally armed with tomahawks and war clubs. They were led by what answered for a band of music, which created what may be termed a discordant din of hideous noises produced by beating on hollow vessels and striking sticks and clubs together. They advanced, not with a regular march, but a continued dance.

* * * * * * * *

The morning was very warm and the perspiration was pouring from them almost in streams. Their eyes were wild and bloodshot. Their countenance had assumed an expression of all the worst passions which can find a place in the breast of the savage—fierce anger, terrible hate, dire revenge, remorseless cruelty—all were expressed in their terrible features. Their muscles stood out in great hard knots, as if wrought to a tension which must burst them. Their tomahawks and clubs were thrown and brandished about in every direction with the most terrible ferocity, and with a force and energy which could only result from the highest excitement, and with every step and every gesture they uttered the most frightful yells, in every imaginable key and note, though generally the highest and shrillest possible. The dance consisted of leaps and spasmodic steps, now forward and now back or sideways, with the whole body distorted in every imaginable unnatural position, most generally stooping forward, with the head and face thrown up, the back arched down, first one foot thrown far forward and then withdrawn, and the other similarly thrust out, frequently squatting quite to the ground and all with a movement almost as quick as lightning. Their weapons were brandished as if they would slay a thousand enemies at every blow, while the yells and screams they uttered were broken up and multiplied and rendered all the more hideous by a rapid clapping of the mouth with the palm of one hand.

To see such an exhibition by a single individual would have been sufficient to excite a sense of fear in a person not overnervous. Five hundred such, all under the influence of the strongest and wildest excitement, constituting a raging sea of dusky painted naked fiends, presented a spectacle absolutely appalling.

When the head of the column had reached the front of the hotel, leaping, dancing, gesticulating, and screaming, while they looked up at the windows, with hell itself depicted on their faces, at the "chemokonian squaws" with which they were filled, and brandishing their weapons as if they were about to make a real attack in deadly earnest, the rear was still on the other side of the river two hundred yards off, and all the intervening space, including the bridge and its approaches, was covered with this raging savagery glistening in the sun, reeking with streamy sweat, fairly frothing at their mouths as with unaffected rage, it seemed as if we had a picture of hell itself before us and a carnival of the damned spirits there confined, whose pastimes we may suppose should present some such scenes as this.

It was well that I was near, and it may well be supposed that she who now looked to me for support and protection clung closer to my side as she breathed short and quick in actual fear. If the other ladies near us had, during the two weeks or more, while the town had been overrun with Indians, become accustomed to look upon their naked bodies and horrid faces, and had acquired a confidence that there was no real danger from their presence, it was not so with her, who had just seen them for the first time and knew nothing of the wild Western Indians but what she had learned of their savage butcheries and tortures in history and legends. The question forced itself on even those who had seen them most, what if they should in their maddened frenzy turn this sham warfare into a real attack? How easy it would be for them to massacre us all, and leave not a living soul to tell the story. Some such remark as this was often heard, and it was not strange if the girl beside me trembled and stood in need of some reassurance and encouragement. She stood it bravely enough and saw the sight to its very end, except that once she retired to her room for a few minutes, but I was not sorry when the last had disappeared around the corner as they passed down Lake Street and only those horrid sounds which reached us told us that the war dance was still progressing.

All men are by nature equally free and have inherent rights. Government is or ought to be instituted for the common benefit and security of the people, nation or community.

James Madison

War involves in its progress such a train of unforeseen circumstances that no human wisdom can calculate the end; it has but one thing certain, and that is to increase taxes.

Thomas Paine

ALBERT SCHWEITZER, M.D.

on the occasion of his 80th birthday, December 1954

by MARION MILL PREMINGER *for*

"WHAT'S NEW," ABBOTT LABORATORIES

ALBERT SCHWEITZER, M.D. Merry Christmas to you and Happy Birthday and many happy returns. You will be eighty next month.

I know that this is your favorite title—although the world gave you more glittering names than you ever had glittering Christmas ornaments on your simple Christmas tree in Lambaréné, Gabon, Equatorial French Africa, where you have spent your last forty Christmases in the middle of a leper colony.

> Americans call you: Number one man in the world
> Britishers call you: The man of the century
> Frenchmen call you: *Le plus grand Français vivant*
> Germans call you: The most remarkable man of the age
> Italians call you: The greatest genius since Leonardo Da Vinci
> Dutch call you: The great men's great man
> Spaniards call you: The greatest humanitarian living
> The natives in French Equatorial Africa call you: The famous unknown

. . . But I who had the privilege to work next to you, I call you: The near saint. Because to watch you as a doctor is to be as near to God as one can get. The century hails you world authority on the music of Johann Sebastian Bach: world authority on the writings of Goethe: world authority on the philosophical writings of Kant: world authority on the preachings of Saint Paul the Apostle. But I, who have had the privilege to live next to you and who saw you work as a simple country doctor, I call you: A world authority on human kindness. You who were an ordained minister and became a medical doctor, to do good and not to preach it: whose hospital is open day and night for the sick, no questions asked: who medicates, nurses, houses, feeds and clothes thousands and thousands of poor natives: who not only fashioned the phrase, "Reverence for Life," but lives it, working sixteen hours a day, even this year—your eightieth.

They call you God's own man, and I am sure you do not realize that you are the human miracle of kindness of this whole century. As I am sure, saints do not know they are saints any more than a giant palm knows high it towers over other trees.

Albert Schweitzer, M.D., who remains unshaken and unimpressed by the doings of others, whose greatness is so big that all the worldly honors from which he hid ran after him and found him deep in the jungle in the sizzling sun of the equator, who by his simple being catalytically shows us that evil is unnatural, his self-forgetting attention to everything living unknowingly teaches us that we all are our brothers' keepers. I call him The Thirteenth Apostle. I hope I go before him, so I can tell the other Twelve Apostles on the other side to have lots and lots of work prepared for him, so that eternity should not look to him like eternity. Because without work he couldn't stand it even in Heaven.

* * * * *

As daughter of a diplomat I have lived on all continents. The number of countries I have traveled in is greater than the number of my years. I have met scores of distinguished and eminent people —heads of states, Nobel Prize winners, scientists, diplomats, educators . . . of all nationalities, all ages, all races. The only personality whose influence on my life is infinite is Dr. Albert Schweitzer.

MARION MILL PREMINGER –

Founder of The Albert Schweitzer Hospital Fund

* * * * *

A new commandment I give unto you, That ye love one another; as I have loved you, that ye also love one another. By this shall all men know that ye are my disciples, if ye have love one to another.
— ST. JOHN *13:34,35*

A GENTLE PHILOSOPHY

From Walden

by HENRY D. THOREAU

Born at Concord, Massachusetts, July 12, 1817, graduated from Harvard, 1837, when he began teaching school and later became a land surveyor. He was a friend of Emerson and other contemporaries and believed strongly in the rights of the individual. He was at one time imprisoned for refusal to pay taxes. Died May 6, 1862.

TIME is but the stream I go a-fishing in. I drink at it; but while I drink I see the sandy bottom and detect how shallow it is. Its thin current slides away, but eternity remains. I would drink deeper; fish in the sky, whose bottom is pebbly with stars. I cannot count one. I know not the first letter of the alphabet. I have always been regretting that I was not as wise as the day I was born. The intellect is a cleaver; it discerns and rifts its way into the secret of things. I do not wish to be any more busy with my hands than is necessary. My head is hands and feet. I feel all my best faculties concentrated in it. My instinct tells me that my head is an organ for burrowing, as some creatures use their snout and forepaws, and with it I would mine and burrow my way through these hills. I think that the richest vein is somewhere hereabouts; so by the divining rod and thin rising vapors I judge; and here I will begin to mine.

If a man does not keep pace with his companions, perhaps it is because he hears a different drummer. Let him step to the music which he hears, however measured or far away.

—HENRY DAVID THOREAU

Business

Labor is in fact a high mission. It is for man, like an effective and intelligent collaboration with God the Creator, from whom man has received the goods of the earth, to cultivate them and make them prosper.

—Pope John XXIII

Never shrink from doing anything honorable which your business calls you to do. The man who is above his business, may one day find his business above him.

Wide is the gate and broad is the way that leadeth to destruction, and many there be which go in thereat:
Because strait is the gate and narrow is the way which leadeth unto life, and few there be that find it.

Matthew VII: 13, 14

War Hero Audie Recalled—and His Views on Bravery

by WILLIAM C. BARNARD

Reprinted by permission of the Associated Press

*When Lieutenant Audie Murphy came home the most deco-
rated United States soldier of World War II in 1945, he expressed these thoughts to William C. Barnard on a long drive
through Texas. After his discharge from the army, he became
a celebrated actor, his best known movies being* Beyond Glory,
The Kid from Texas, Red Badge of Courage, The Unforgiven,
To Hell and Back, Night Passage, Destry, *and* Arizona Raiders.
He died in the crash of a chartered plane on May 31, 1971.

THIRTEEN U.S. generals flew in from Europe that summer day of 1945, landing at San Antonio, Texas. The whole
line of them descended from the C-54 transport into the
warm ranks of a reception committee.

Then, right behind the generals came this freckle-faced
kid, fresh from European battlefields, limping down the
ramp because of wounds in both legs and his hip. He was
5 feet 5 inches tall and weighed 134 pounds. He was twenty
but he looked seventeen or less. He was so shy he didn't give
his name to a single member of the welcoming committee.

Won every medal

But reporters recognized him and promptly forgot the
thirteen generals they had come to interview. For this was
Audie L. Murphy, the most decorated soldier in United
States history. He had won every combat decoration the
United States offers, including the Silver Star twice.

This was Murphy who won the Medal of Honor, the nation's highest military honor, with a lone, victorious stand
on a blazing tank destroyer against 250 German infantry-

men and six German tanks. Here was Murphy and he didn't smoke, drink or cuss. He looked like an Eagle Scout.

San Antonio went wild when it found Murphy was back in Texas. So did Dallas. Officials chartered a plane to fly him to Dallas the next morning and parade him to his Farmersville home where fire trucks would be waiting to lead the welcome. It was a royal homecoming for a green-eyed kid who had to start earning his living at twelve.

He gets a lift

I had been to Farmersville and had met his older sister and his two younger sisters and his little brother, so I got him aside and told him news of his family. He was hungry for this news.

"I'll see you at Farmersville tomorrow," I told Audie. "How are you travelin'?"

"I have a car and plan to leave at 6 A.M."

"Pick me up at 6:05," said Murphy. "I'll be on the corner across the street from the hotel."

"You can't do that," I said. "All sorts of plans are in the works for you."

The missing hero

"I'll tell 'em I have changed the plans," Murphy said firmly.

"See you at 6:05."

He was there, all right, and we started out for the northern Texas agricultural community of Farmersville, three hundred miles away. Two hours later Murphy humorously confessed he hadn't called anyone to report his change in plans. When I finally got to a phone, I found there was considerable concern about the disappearance of the war hero.

But Murphy was thoroughly relaxed. As we drove along, his vision followed the passing scene, green rows of corn, gentle hills, fat cattle in the soft tree shade of a meadow.

"This is what I came home to see," Murphy said. "You can't realize how swell this is. Over there it was a helluva thing. There were times our outfit was in battle seventy to eighty days without relief. You got mad and disgusted and you didn't care what happened to you. This was the way I felt on that tank destroyer."

He stopped talking, to watch a tractor running down the rows of a cotton field.

Bravery defined

"They talk about bravery," he resumed. "Well, I'll tell you what bravery really is. Bravery is just determination to do a job that you know has to be done. If you throw in discomforts and lack of sleep and anger, it is easier to be brave.

"Just wanting to be back in a country like this can make a man brave. I have seen many a doughfoot do many a brave thing because he wanted to get the war over with in a hurry and go home. Many a guy who wanted to come home worse than anything else in the world will stay over there forever. They are the fellows I want the honors to go to, not to me."

Murphy pointed across a sunny field.

"This is enough for me," he said.

Let me but live my life from year to year,
    With forward face and unreluctant soul.
    Not hurrying to, nor turning from the goal;
Not mourning for the things that disappear
In the dim past, nor holding back in fear
    From what the future veils; but with a whole
    And happy heart, that pays its toll
To youth and age, and travels on with cheer.

— HENRY VAN DYKE

MARRIED TO A GRAPE NUT

by Erma Bombeck

Courtesy of Publishers–Hall Syndicate

I F THERE is anything to match the old male ego, I don't know what it is.

The other night, we ordered wine at dinner The waiter proceeded to pour a capful in a glass for my husband to approve or disapprove.

Right away, he's Cesar Romero. First, he makes a circle with the glass under his nose. Then he tilts back his head like he is going to make Jeane Dixon materialize. Finally, his tongue touches the wine.

The rest of us at the table sit there like idiots waiting for this man who doesn't know a vintage port from last week's Kool-Aid to decide whether or not the wine will meet with his favor or disfavor.

The waiter shifts his weight to the other foot. Finally, Cesar speaks. "A bit more please," he says, extending his glass. As my eyes roll back in my head, he says, "I've got to be sure."

"You have not the foggiest notion what you are doing," I accused.

"Why would you make a statement like that?" he asks.

"Because I have that same look on my face when I squeeze melons in the supermarket, and I don't have the foggiest notion of what I am doing."

"For your information, my dear," he says, wiping a bit of the grape off his chin, "tasting wine is an old tradition that was initiated to protect kings and queens from being poisoned."

"Where were you when the pot roast was served?" I asked dryly.

As he sat there smacking his lips and wrestling with his Minnie Mouse decision, another question crossed my mind. How does the waiter know which one to have sample the wine for the rest of the group? The one with the reddest nose? (Lay it on Rudolph, Harvey, he's had the most experience.) Or the one who looks like he's going to pay the check? Or the Secret Service type who goes around protecting kings and queens.

"By the way," I finally said to my husband. "You've sampled half the bottle. Do you suppose it is safe for the rest of us to have a little wine for our dinner?"

"I sent that particular bottle back," he said.

"You're kidding. Why?"

"Why indeed. You're not fooling around with some little old lady who only tipples at the faculty Christmas party. I've had wine many times before in my home. I ordered them to serve us Lake Erie 1970, and this time, I want to see cork floating around in it!"

For "Is" and "Is-NOT" though with Rule
  and Line
And "UP-AND-DOWN" by Logic I define,
  Of all that one should care to fathom, I
Was never deep in anything but—Wine.

The Grape that can with Logic absolute
The Two-and-Seventy jarring Sects con-
  fute:
  The subtle Alchemist that in a Trice
Life's leaden Metal into Gold transmute.

RUBÁIYÁT OF OMAR KHAYYÁM

FAITH—

MOST IMPORTANT INGREDIENT
IN OUR SUCCESS

by

Eugene Whitmore

Business history proves that the people who have the most to gain from a new development are frequently the first and most vigorous opponents of the idea. It also proves that had the typical business pioneer listened to his financial backers, his board of directors or other intimate associates he would have abandoned his idea before it got off the ground.

When Cyrus H. K. Curtis was building the circulation of the Ladies' Home Journal the Philadelphia advertising agency of N. W. Ayer & Son sold him an extensive advertising campaign which pushed the circulation to the then unheard of total of 100,000 copies a month.

Encouraged by this success Curtis outlined his plans to Mr. Ayer for even greater expansion. Ayer told him that he would need bank credit and credit from a big paper mill. He asked Curtis how much credit would be needed.

"Two hundred thousand dollars," explained Curtis. This seems like petty cash when considered against today's millions required for a national magazine. Curtis showed so much enthusiasm and confidence in his ability to expand Ayer agreed to help him obtain credit.

The two men went to Boston to visit Crocker, Burbank & Company, owners of large paper mill properties. The owners of the paper mill had been notified in advance of the visit of Ayer and Curtis. When they arrived they were greeted with typical New England courtesy, reserved but friendly. Then they were told that it was useless to discuss

We walk by faith, not by sight.

II Corinthians V:7

credits as it had already been decided that the paper company could not consider extending credit for six months, and for $100,000.

Curtis outlined his plans for expanding his publishing enterprise. Although his efforts proved futile as far as the paper mill owners were concerned his enthusiasm kindled a fire in the mind of Mr. Ayer. When it was obvious that the paper makers were determined to refuse credit Mr. Curtis was asked to leave the room for a few moments. When he returned the paper makers told him they had changed their minds; the credit would be granted.

Curtis returned to Philadelphia and pushed the circulation of the Ladies' Home Journal so rapidly that many new advertisers were attracted. He paid the paper bills as they came due.

Then he purchased the moribund Saturday Evening Post for $1,000 because of its name and because it had once been published by Benjamin Franklin. Nearly everybody in the publishing, advertising and paper business predicted that he would soon lose all the money he had made from the Ladies' Home Journal on the feeble weekly he had purchased. But Curtis had big plans. He went to the same Boston paper makers and asked for six months credit.

After long discussions behind closed doors Curtis obtained credit for a six month supply of paper. At the end of six months the money to pay the notes was not available. He went to Boston again, for another selling job on the paper makers. Some members of the firm were opposed to granting him any more credit, but finally he succeeded in winning over two younger members of the firm. They convinced the older men that the Curtis business should be accepted—on credit, for another six months.

Curtis promised that this accommodation would never be forgotten, and predicted that Crocker, Burbank would grow along with the Curtis Publishing Company. Both Curtis magazines prospered, and Crocker, Burbank added huge papermaking machines to take care of the Curtis contract.

The wise man must be wise before, not after, the event.
Fabulae Incertae, EPICHARMUS

For thirty-four years thereafter Curtis bought paper from Crocker, Burbank until it became necessary to find new production where more water was available. Gradually Curtis financed other paper mills, or established its own mills and Crocker, Burbank relinquished the business to care for other customers.

Years after Curtis was a prompt paying customer of Crocker, Burbank and was using all the paper the company could produce one of the paper makers told him that his first credit was granted only because Mr. Ayer agreed to guarantee payment of the notes.

Had it not been for the selling job Curtis did on Mr. Ayer, had not Ayer agreed to guarantee payment there probably would be no Ladies' Home Journal, as we know it today, and no Saturday Evening Post.

Only supreme faith in his own ability could have convinced Ayer, who had seen many publications fail, that the ideas of Mr. Curtis were worth backing with heavy financial commitments. Yet the people who had so much to gain from the Curtis orders for paper backed away from the opportunity and required a guarantee from a third party before accepting the business.

No enterprise succeeds without great faith—the sort of faith which sets other men on fire with enthusiasm and confidence. Almost no great enterprise ever enjoys smooth sailing in its early history and the records of business are jammed with accounts of early failures because somebody lacked faith to go ahead.

Several early stockholders in the Ford Motor Company sold stock which later would have made them multi-millionaires had they kept faith and retained their stock.

Make fools believe in their foreseeing
Of things before they are in being;
To swallow gudgeons ere they're catch'd,
And count their chickens ere they're hatch'd.

Hudibras, SAMUEL BUTLER

Perseverence, dear my lord, Keeps honor bright.

Troilus and Cressida, WILLIAM SHAKESPEARE

A College Boy's Idea

Launched 22,000 Business Enterprises

by EUGENE WHITMORE

CHARLES MARTIN HALL, a 22 year old graduate of Oberlin College in Ohio discovered, in 1886, a commercially successful method of extracting alumina from common ore bearing clay. From this alumina he produced the light metal we call aluminum.

Hall was confident that a huge market awaited this strong, light, bright, rustproof metal. For two years he mowed lawns, trimmed hedges and sold books from house to house to finance his effort to find investors to finance a small plant.

On a hot day in July 1888 a friend sent Hall to Captain Alfred E. Hunt, a Pittsburgh metallurgical engineer. After one or two meetings Captain Hall agreed to organize a company and obtain $20,000 to finance a plant.

By February 1889, before the plant was completed Hall wrote his sister saying: "We have already made away with $18,000." Only a few ingots had been produced.

To shore up the company's finances Captain Hall sailed to England in search of British investors. One company seemed interested and engaged a famous engineering company to advise them. Among other things the engineering report declared:

"One ton of aluminum, if it could be produced, would supply the world's demand for a full year."

Hall returned to Pittsburgh without money. The little company owed $4,000 and had no money to pay the debt. Hunt tried to borrow from several banks, but got only cold turn-downs. Then a friend sent him to the T. Mellon & Sons Bank. Late one afternoon Hunt got in to see Andrew Mellon who listened courteously while Hunt detailed the

There is no sanctuary so holy that money cannot profane it, no fortress so strong that money cannot take it by storm.

—In Verrem, CICERO

company's dire financial straights. Although called the Pittsburgh Reduction Company the plant and office were in a small iron-clad shed on Pittsburgh's Smallman street, and was anything but impressive.

Mellon gave no encouragement and did not commit his bank in any way, but told Hunt to return the following day. Hunt spent a sleepless night worrying about the outcome of his interview with Mr. Mellon.

Next day he called on Mellon again. Although Hunt did not know it, Andrew and his brother R. B. Mellon had inspected the little plant the very afternoon Hunt had first called. Mr. Mellon told Hunt.

"You need considerably more than the $4,000 to pay the loan."

Hunt probably gulped and steadied himself for another turndown. But Mr. Mellon went on to say that he would loan the $4,000 to pay the note and advance more funds for working capital.

From that day on the company we now know of as Aluminum Corporation of America had no more financial difficulties. Soon Captain Hunt engaged the son of a friend to work in the company, a man named Arthur Vining Davis who soon was in full charge of the company, and who remained with the company until his retirement after World War II.

As many other pioneers had in the past, the young men in charge of the aluminum company soon found that they could produce the metal much faster than anybody wanted to buy it. A few pounds were sold here and there to jewelry manufacturers, novelty companies, and to utensil manufacturers who experimented with the metal, but continued to stick to cast and enameled iron or brass.

> *Money is like manure, of very little use*
> *except it be spread.*
> *—Apothegms,* SIR FRANCIS BACON

At first each new ingot that came from the plant was stored in the small safe in the office. Soon the safe was too small to hold the production. Davis heard of a big power project in California and hurried there to sell aluminum wire, which conducts electricity as well as copper and is much lighter.

Davis obtained the order and hoped to turn it over to some established steel or copper wire company for production. No one wanted the order. The old, established wire companies refused even to make a trial run of aluminum wire. To save this order Davis promptly built a wire mill and filled the order.

Customers were slow in learning to use aluminum, and many established manufacturers refused to try the light metal. At one time Mr. Davis tried to sell the Griswold Company of Erie, Pennsylvania on the idea of putting a cast aluminum tea kettle in their line of cast iron skillets and other utensils. Mr. Davis borrowed a skilled iron moulder from Griswold and established him in a plant at New Kensington to prove that a cast aluminum kettle was feasible. The Griswold people approved the kettles turned out by their moulder, but refused to entertain the idea of manufacturing them, although he gave Davis an order for 2,000 kettles, which Davis promptly put into production.

A Massachusetts company which had been buying sheet aluminum from the company for use in making utensils went bankrupt and settled its account with the aluminum company (still known as Pittsburgh Reduction Company) by turning over its equipment and orders to them.

Invention is the talent of youth, and judgment of age.

—Jonathan Swift

One order for 2,800 kettles was found among the company papers. Officials of the Pittsburgh company, intrigued by such a large order sent for the young men whose company had ordered the 2,800 kettles. When they arrived in Pittsburgh it developed that the young men, J. H. Wilson and Charles E. Ziegler had paid their way through college selling utensils house to house. They had then formed a company to sell utensils which they bought from the Massachusetts company which had failed. They were looking for a new source of supply. The aluminum men were looking for somebody who knew how to sell. A deal was made and the two young men joined with Pittsburgh Reduction Company to organize a force of house to house salesmen. In a few years the Aluminum Cooking Utensil Company was formed to market Wear-ever cooking utensils and from three to five thousand college men spent their summer vacations selling aluminum utensils.

One of these young salesmen later became a partner of J. P. Morgan & Company, others went on to careers in law, medicine and other professions, while some built successful careers in merchandising aluminum products.

By 1900 aluminum was catching on as a valuable raw material for many products, and soon a veritable "aluminum craze" swept the country. Hundreds of companies were formed to make all sorts of items of aluminum. The company itself brought out aluminum horseshoes and just when they were winning acceptance the automobile industry began putting horses and mules out to pasture.

The Wright Brothers used sheet aluminum in the first plane they flew at Kitty Hawk, North Carolina. A pullman car was made of aluminum. Many uses for it were found by

He that voluntarily continues in ignorance,
is guilty of all the crimes which ignorance produces.
—Letter to Mr. W. Drummond, SAMUEL JOHNSON

the automobile industry. Truck bodies, boats, airplanes, barns were built of aluminum; siding for residences was developed. Some bicycles were built of aluminum. At different times many companies attempted to use aluminum for purposes for which it was unsuited.

Without aluminum the great aviation industry might not have developed. One item at a time the company began producing wire, sheets, castings, moulding, rods, plates and practically every product produced by other metal companies.

Today more than 22,000 shops, factories, mills and processing plants fabricate or handle aluminum as a major raw material. And it all started when a college boy succeeded, after several years of dangerous experimenting and nearly burning down his parents' home, in obtaining the metal from common clay.

Charles Martin Hall did not live to see many spectacular developments of the industry he founded, yet he was a wealthy man at his death. Arthur Vining Davis, one of the company's first employees became wealthy, piloted the company through multi-million dollar expansions and two world wars, then retired, moved to Florida and entered into large scale land clearing and housing developments.

One idea, several determined young salesmen and a world of persistence created an industry to serve the world, employ thousands of people, and enrich thousands of business enterprises.

Yet the pioneers of the business never forget that one of the world's most prominent engineering firms declared that one ton of aluminum would supply the entire world for a full year.

He that shall endure unto the end the same shall be saved.
—St. Matthew X, 22

THE CHEESE PEDDLER
WITH BIG IDEAS
By Eugene Whitmore

W HEN J. L. KRAFT obtained a job in a small grocery store in Canada somebody jokingly told him that he would receive his first raise in salary when he learned to slice off half pound wedges of cheese accurately.

In those days no package cheese was available. Cheese came in big "wheels" and the grocer did a masterful job of guessing when a customer asked for half a pound of cheese; sometimes the grocer got the better of the deal and at other times the customer obtained an ounce or two extra because it was not customary to trim the original slice, or to add another slice if the scales showed that the big wedge of cheese was over or under weight.

This guesswork bothered Kraft. He thought cheese should be accurately weighed and put up in neat, individual packages which would preserve the product's flavor, moisture and taste and deliver it to the customer "untouched by human hands."

Kraft thought that his plan was sound, both for the dealer and the customer. It insured better quality, more accurate weights and vastly improved sanitation.

No one seemed interested in Kraft's idea. Cheese had *always* been packed in these big wheels; it would be too much trouble for the cheese makers to pack cheese in small, convenient units. Besides it would cost too much. Kraft maintained that the loss from drying out, the loss from careless cutting and weighing, and the waste from spoilage would more than offset the small extra cost of individual packages.

The more Kraft tried to interest people in his idea the more they opposed it. He kept on thinking about it until the idea of cheese in small, sanitary packages became almost an obsession with him. He quit his job, moved from Canada to Chicago.

Or thinke, that the moone is made of a greene cheese.
—Epigrams and Proverbs, JOHN HEYWOOD

After continued discouragement and constant ridicule of his idea Kraft set himself up in a tiny room on Chicago's old Water Street, where the city's produce and perishable foods were handled. He bought the big wheels of cheese, sliced them into small, accurately weighed units and put the small units into individually wrapped packages.

When he tried to interest wholesalers in handling his products they laughed at him; brokers thought the idea ridiculous and told him so. After all the negative advice he received Kraft should have, by all the rules of logic, shut up his little shop, forgotten his idea and gone to work for somebody else.

Instead of quitting he started out to sell direct to grocery stores. With a basket of packaged cheese over each arm Kraft started out each morning peddling his cheese packages, a few at a time to any store owner he could sell. Sometimes he would return to try and sell a repeat order and find none of his cheese had been sold. But he continued to preach his gospel of cheese in small, sanitary packages until a few stores began to build some trade on it.

He worked at night packaging the cheese; after a long time he saved enough money to buy a horse and wagon. His horse was named Paddy and before long was a familiar sight on certain Chicago streets. Gradually his business increased. Kraft hired a salesman, bought another horse and wagon. It looked as if his idea was catching on. Right when prospects brightened, on the very second day that both his wagons were on the streets, a trolley car and one horse and wagon collided and the Kraft cheese wagon and horse came off definitely second best. The horse had to be destroyed and the wagon was wrecked beyond repair.

As a lyke to compare in taste, chalk and cheese.
—Proverbs, JOHN HEYWOOD

On the following day old Paddy—good old Paddy—laid down and died. Kraft was back on foot, a basket over each arm, once more peddling cheese to his customers. A proud man, Kraft had taken a lot of abuse and ridicule from some grocery merchants. One in particular thought the idea of selling cheese in small individually wrapped packages was little short of insane. During an argument one day this grocer, who had the best trade in Chicago, told Kraft to "get out and stay out."

Meanwhile his trade was growing. He acquired more horses and more wagons and had an established trade in some stores. Then, out of a blue sky, so to speak, this crusty grocer, who had once ordered Kraft out of his store, sent word for Kraft to call on him, saying that he wanted to stock Kraft cheese products.

Kraft knew that his products were getting established when this call came, and although he needed the business from this prestige account he was human enough to tell that grocer "where he could go." He refused to call on the snooty grocer, explaining that he could well afford to get along without his business.

Practically every man, woman and child in America today knows the remainder of this story. Kraft Foods, as the company is now called is housed in a big private office building on Chicago's lake front. The company owns processing plants in many parts of the country and produces or processes a long line of food products.

Mr. Kraft retired some years ago, but his spirit lingers on because his success, after heart-breaking discouragement, is proof that it pays to hang onto a good idea, to have faith in self, and to snap your fingers in the face of even the direst adversity.

*Faith is the substance of things, hoped for,
the evidence of things not seen.*

—Hebrews **XI,** 1

Today there are many thousand Kraft customers who now buy each year much more than the total sales of Kraft cheese to all customers back in the early days of the business. Some of these customers, whose purchases run into the millions probably never have learned that the great Kraft food enterprise was started by one man, walking along Chicago's streets, with two baskets on his arms, selling a few dollars worth of cheese at a time.

Here is a typically American story of courage, enterprise, persistence and final victory against odds that would discourage all but the stoutest hearts. Somewhere in America today, probably in some little corner store, or tiny shop, other men are developing ideas, dreaming dreams, putting down the roots of enterprises which will, in time, produce and sell in multi-million brackets.

The piper he piped on the hill top high
"Butter and eggs and a pound of cheese,"
Till the cow said, "I die," and the goose said, "Why?"
And the dog said nothing, but searched for fleas.
        —*Ballad of the Period,* CHARLES S. CALVERLEY

BUILDING MEN

by

Robert W. Murphy

How do you train him?
There he stands before you,
Clean and lanky,
With a look of bright morning on his face.
Appealing
In the way that morning is,
And youth is,
And the hopefulness of youth.

And then you realize
The awful responsibility
That is yours
To train.
To train and build,
And nurture and lead.
You realize how much of business is training,
How much of modern industry is building men,
Inspiring men,
And leading them to achievement.

Well, here is good timber
But what are you going to build of it?
And how do you go about the building process?

This is the answer:
You give him of yourself.

Urge him learn his craft of course,
And learn it well,
Whatever it is — law, accounting, engineering.

Tell him he must labor hard, to learn it well.
That, of course,
Goad him to dip into classic tomes
And newer letters
To touch base often
In academic halls
And move about in tasks foreign and unfamiliar.

But this young man needs more.
Judgment he needs,
And understanding,
And maturity.

For these, he looks to you
And you must give them to him.

Let yourself rub off on him,
Let him sit beside you as you work,
To work with you,
To study with you,
To be perplexed with you,
To analyze with you,
And to dream with you.

Give him the impossible task to do,
The unanswerable question to answer.
There is no better way to train —
Whether you be Socrates training Athenian youth,
Or an American man of business
Teaching some young hopeful the craft of management
In mid-century industrial America.

For just experience tells in every soil,
That those who think must govern those who toil.

Traveller, **OLIVER GOLDSMITH**